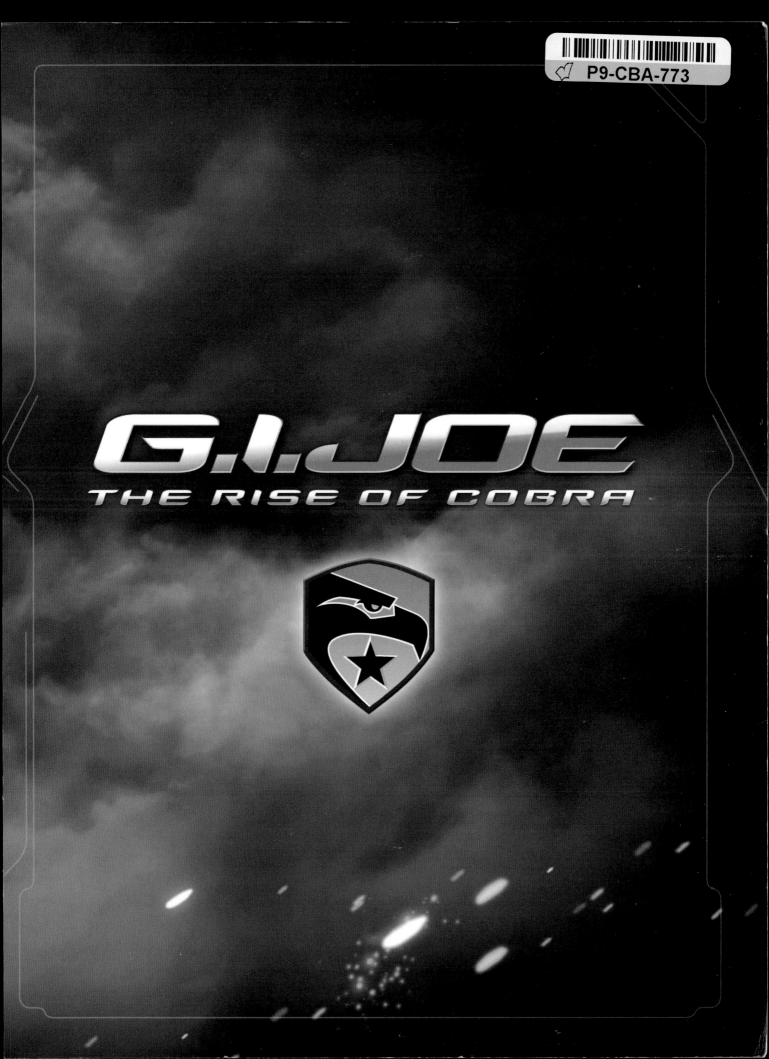

G.I. JOE:
The Rise Of Cobra: Mission Dossier
ISBN 9781848562448

Published by
Titan Books
A division of
Titan Publishing Group Ltd
144 Southwark Street
London
SE1 0UP

First edition July 2009
10 9 8 7 6 5 4 3 2 1

Visit our website:
www.titanbooks.com

ACKNOWLEDGEMENTS
My deepest gratitude goes out to the cast and crew of *G.I. JOE: The Rise of Cobra*, the staff at Titan Books, Hasbro's G.I. JOE brand team, and the Paramount Licensing Group for all their hard work and assistance in creating this book. Special thanks to Riki Leigh Arnold, Joanna Boylett, Jennifer Calzacorto, Wayne Charness, Lorenzo di Bonaventura, Bob Ducsay, Brian Goldner, Christina Hahni, Erik Howsam, Risa Kessler, Ryan Landels, Ngoc Nguyen, Kirsti Payne, Linda Pianigiani, Ben Samuels, Stephen Sommers, Phyllis Ungerleider, Katy Wild.

Titan Books would like to thank the cast and crew of *G.I. JOE: The Rise of Cobra*, in particular Erik Howsam for his time and patience and Stephen Sommers, as well as everyone at Paramount. Special thanks also go to Risa Kessler.

A CIP catalogue record for this title is available from the British Library.

Printed and bound in the United States of America.

To receive advance information, news, competitions, and exclusive Titan offers online, please register as a member by clicking the "sign up" button on our website: www.titanbooks.com
   Did you enjoy this book? We love to hear from our readers. Please e-mail us at: readerfeedback@titanemail.com or write to Reader Feedback at the above address.

G.I. JOE
THE RISE OF COBRA

MISSION DOSSIER

PAUL RUDITIS

TITAN BOOKS

Contents

G.I. JOE:
From Twelve Inches to Thirty-Five Millimeters

The four versions of the G.I. JOE action figure "fighting man" along with the first black G.I JOE.

Hasbro Toys ushered in a new era for boys' toys in 1964 with the introduction of G.I. JOE: America's Moveable Fighting Man. Developed by licensing agent Stan Weston under the guidance of Hasbro's creative director Don Levine, G.I. JOE was the first poseable twelve-inch "doll" intended for a young male audience.

"When Hasbro introduced G.I. JOE back in 1964 it invented the 'action figure,'" Hasbro CEO Brian Goldner explains. "It was a totally new term and concept to people. Prior to that, there were fashion dolls, but the Hasbro team developing G.I. JOE realized that little boys would never play with 'fashion dolls.' So this idea of an 'action figure' and 'action hero' was developed and it really struck a chord with boys around the world."

G.I. JOE started his life with four versions of the "fighting man," one for each branch of the service (army, navy, marine corps, air force), with each sporting the signature facial scar. The toy, along with his

vehicles and accessories, quickly became a huge success. Over the next few years the line grew to include different versions of G.I. JOE, including a black G.I. JOE in select markets and a licensed spin-off figure in Britain called Action Man.

By 1968 sales began to weaken for G.I. JOE, as they did across the board for military-themed toys. Wanting to keep up with the changing political climate, Hasbro shifted G.I. JOE from a military man to an adventurer, branding the entire line of related products as an "Adventure Team" in the early seventies. During this time, G.I. JOE also sported his famed "life-like hair" and a "Kung Fu grip."

G.I. JOE experienced a growth in popularity that could only be thwarted by the energy crisis of the mid-seventies. By 1976 the cost of the petroleum required to make the twelve-inch plastic figure had become increasingly expensive, and production of G.I. JOE was scaled back. But a big change in the industry would encourage a resurgence.

The early seventies "Adventure Team" with "life-like hair" and a "Kung Fu grip."

"G.I. JOE took on a whole new look and 3.75 inch size in the early 1980s," says Goldner. "That smaller G.I. JOE was truly reflective of the time. Back in the late seventies, *Star Wars* had successfully launched and, for the first time, utilized an action figure that was 3.75 inches in size. All of a sudden boys could not only have a more immersive experience, but they could afford to collect many more vehicles and figures and build an entire 'world.'"

America's Moveable Fighting Man became a team of men and women defending against an evil terrorist organization with cutting-edge weapons and diabolical plans. Each member of this heroic team, code named G.I. JOE, had his or her own area of expertise. Hasbro introduced file cards on the back of the toy packaging detailing just who these JOEs were; information that grew from the mythology Hasbro developed with the help of a comic book line created by Larry Hama for Marvel Comics.

"[Hasbro] had drawings of what the figures were supposed to look like," Larry Hama recalls of the meeting where he was introduced to the new version of G.I. JOE. "There would be this guy with a rifle, and it said 'Infantry' about him. There was this girl with a crossbow, and it said 'Intelligence.' It had a guy with a black mask, and it said 'Covert Operations.'"

Of course, the girl with a crossbow became Scarlett and the guy with a black mask evolved into one of the most popular characters in G.I. JOE history, Snake-Eyes.

Not only did Hama work with Hasbro to give all the characters names, but he created an enemy for this team, naming them Cobra.

"I remember handing in the script on the first issue and thinking, 'That's it. That's all the story I've got.'" Hama says. "I felt that way every month. I never thought I had another issue until I actually sat down and did it."

But Hama did continue to create those issues and develop new G.I. JOE characters. The original *G.I. JOE* comic book series ran for 155 issues and spawned a weekday syndicated cartoon series called *G.I. JOE: A Real American Hero.*

"That was the time at which G.I. JOE soared to new heights," Brian Goldner adds. "The eighties G.I. JOE eclipsed the success that the brand enjoyed in the sixties."

This incarnation of G.I. JOE continued to sell over the next two decades with some minor brand changes while remaining true to the core team. The new millennium brought another significant change to the property as part of an overall approach to the entire line of Hasbro products.

"We took a look at all of the great brands in our vast portfolio and thought about how we could re-imagine and re-invent our brands for today's global market," Goldner recalls. "We began with where we had been historically strong, and the boys' business was certainly one of our areas of strength. We had brands like Transformers and G.I. JOE, so we started to focus in on: What kinds of stories could we tell in all forms of media relevant to our consumers today? Of course, motion pictures are right there at the top of the list."

There had been interest in the property from the movie industry over the years, but things did not really get moving until Hasbro teamed up with film producer Lorenzo di Bonaventura. Then the concept for a *G.I. JOE* movie began a long development period that was greatly aided by the success of another Hasbro toy turned film, *Transformers*.

"*Transformers* really helped us get *G.I. JOE* going," di Bonaventura admits, "because the tone and the attitude of this comic book was something a lot of people who had control over 'yes' and 'no' couldn't get their heads around completely [before that movie]. The success of *Transformers* was like, 'Oh, I see. I've got it. This tone of reality and fantasy can mix really well together.' The result of that was we got *G.I. JOE* going, and Paramount has been an unbelievably supportive studio of it."

Not only did the movie get going, it went right into high speed in 2007. With a looming Writers Guild of America strike and the potential for an actors strike, *G.I. JOE: The Rise of Cobra* was quickly put into pre-production. It helped greatly that the production had the contained frenetic energy of the director of the first two films in *The*

The eighties team.

G.I. JOE: The Rise of Cobra's Scarlett and Duke and their eighties action figure counterparts.

Mummy franchise, Stephen Sommers, and his producing partner, Bob Ducsay, onboard. Both men had played with the twelve-inch figure during their childhoods. In fact, this was not producer Bob Ducsay's first brush with the concept of putting G.I. JOE on film.

"When I was a little kid I would make these Super 8 movies—I always had a real interest in making films—and I made a number of G.I. JOE-oriented movies with G.I. JOEs being the key players," Ducsay fondly remembers. "They were my actors."

However, the new film would have a slightly higher budget and focus not on the twelve-inch figure but on the newer characters from the eighties—which led to some initial confusion on the part of director Stephen Sommers.

"When I first heard about the G.I. JOE movie, I thought it was an army man movie," he admits. "I didn't really have any ideas for it and was not that interested in it. They'd done a couple of scripts and I read those scripts and they were very generic action movies. But my assistant and my producing partner's assistant, they love the G.I. JOE of the last twenty-five years. They started talking about Snake-Eyes and Storm Shadow and Scarlett and the Baroness and educating me on the whole thing. Then I got really excited because I suddenly saw the potential. Especially with the two women. I thought I could have romances, and strong women characters. I love doing romantic movies—romantic adventures, romantic action, romantic comedy—all that stuff."

With those thoughts in mind, Sommers got down to business embracing the property. "I read everything," he excitedly admits, "and I saw everything. I just loved it because there was so much to draw from.

It's a huge palette with all these great back-stories and interweaving relationships. They were great characters, great relationships, and I just fell in love with all that."

The first big challenge they encountered was the sheer logistics involved in bringing such beloved characters to the screen. Considering that approximately ninety percent of the audience for the *Transformers* movie were people who were not familiar with the cartoon, the production had to walk a delicate line between creating a *G.I. JOE* movie that would appeal to a new audience while not alienating the legions of fans. This was especially clear from the fact that the main question anyone involved with the production would hear from those not "in the know" was, "Who's playing G.I. JOE?"

The decision was made to make the movie an origin story, introducing the audience to the concept of G.I. JOE through the characters of Duke and Ripcord. Brian Goldner served as a producer to ensure that everyone stayed true to the brand. His company's involvement was very much welcomed by the production.

"Hasbro is a great company to work with," di Bonaventura proclaims, "because all the people internally are fans. So they approach the subject matter as a fan does. It makes it a lot easier to be true to the property because the company has the same agenda as the fan would have."

Ducsay sums up the relationship between the production and Hasbro more succinctly: "They're toymakers, so how could they be anything but fun?"

But di Bonaventura already had an ace in the hole with executive producer Erik Howsam, an unabashed fan of the eighties' incarnation who had every intention of making sure the film stayed true to the original.

"My job as a fan was to try to hew as closely as I could to the property as I knew it," Howsam confirms. "Even when there were interpretations going on, I would be the one who would say, 'Wait a second. Snake-Eyes doesn't do that,' or 'Storm Shadow doesn't do that.' Because I grew up with it and I knew it.

"I think in some ways you have to grow up and know it; to remember how you felt when you were a twelve-year-old boy, seeing it for the first time. You were passionate about what you were watching and what you were reading. Those storylines and those character dynamics, they mean a lot. If you start messing around with that stuff too much, then it's sort of: Why are you making a movie called *G.I. JOE*?"

With those fans in mind, the production staff began the intricate process of laying out the world of the movie. The first step was choosing who from among the battalion of G.I. JOE characters would make it into the film.

"It is a complicated process," Bob Ducsay says. "Part of it comes as you start developing the scenario of what the story is. As soon as you do that, you go, 'Which characters will fit into that scenario?' Then it's a little bit of a push/pull between, 'We really love these characters, they would be great to put in the first movie,' versus, 'How do these characters fit into the story that we want to tell?'

"There were obvious things. You don't even have to think that Snake-Eyes is in the movie. And Storm Shadow is in the movie. Then after that you have to start thinking about which of the characters in this rich tapestry you *really* want to use. That's the reason that we came up with the characters that ended up in the movie."

Every step of the way, the production consulted Hasbro as well as the comic book creator, Larry Hama. "Our model is, 'Larry's happy, we're happy,'" di Bonaventura says. "And so far, so good. The thing that we've constantly felt about this property is, they created something really interesting, why muck it up? Larry is there as our sounding board."

Larry Hama takes his role as quality control very seriously. But he

is also realistic about the needs of creating a movie for a broad audience. "You have to make compromises for myriads of reasons just to get it done," Hama explains. "But if the intrinsic center of it—the core—is still true, then it's really the same thing."

The film is an ensemble piece true to those core characters and beliefs of G.I. JOE, both old and new. The complete G.I. JOE unit has evolved, becoming a group of international heroes reflecting the times we live in, while Duke's character serves as a callback to the original "Government Issued JOE"—right down to the scar under his eye—as well as being the embodiment of the All American Hero namesake character from the eighties incarnation. But, whether a die-hard fan or a newcomer to the brand, *G.I. JOE: The Rise of Cobra* is a movie made for the kid in all of us.

"I was basically pinching myself every day," Erik Howsam's inner-child reveals. "I know it's a cliché to say when you just love something so much, but it was amazing…. To be standing next to Snake-Eyes and Storm Shadow, and really playing a part in deciding who was cast in each role, what they looked like and what characters were in the movie—it was fantastic. It really was the ultimate high."

"I think the people who grew up with this version of G.I. JOE—I'll be shocked if they're not thrilled. And then everybody else, because it is an origin story, it opens it up to everybody," says director Sommers of his belief that the movie will be embraced by existing G.I. JOE fans, while also finding new ones. "Even if they've never heard of Snake-Eyes, they will get to see where he came from and who he is, and by the end of the movie, I think he'll be their favorite character. That's the key. I hope it will open it up to a whole new audience."

And producer di Bonaventura believes that, whether for old fans or new, the movie is going to be a huge adventure.

"We're going for it. There's no stunt that we won't go for. There's no joke that we won't reach for. There's no dramatic element that we won't go full-steam for, and keep going until we get it."

Yo JOE! ★

Channing Tatum and Lorenzo di Bonaventura.

Stephen Sommers and Ray Park.

0° 30° 60° 90° 120° 15

Greenland Sea

Norwegian Sea

RUSSIA

Sea of Okhot

SWEDEN

FINLAND

Gulf
of
Bothnia

North Sea

DENMARK

Baltic Sea

POLAND

BYELORUS

CONVOY ASSAULT
41°13'05N 74°46'11E
ACCESS FILE

English Channel

IRELAND

U.K.

NETH

GERMANY

LUX

CZECH

UKRAINE

KAZAKH

MONGOLIA

Bay of Biscay

FRANCE

ITALY

MOLDOVA

ROMANIA

Caspian
Sea

KYRGYZSTAN

Black Sea

PORTUGAL

SPAIN

GREECE

TURKEY

AZERBAIJAN

TURKMENISTAN

CHINA

NORTH KOREA

Sea of
Japan

SOUTH KOREA

JAPAN

Mediterranean Sea

SYRIA

IRAQ

IRAN

PAKISTAN

East China
Sea

TUNISIA

ISRAEL

North Pa

MOROCCO

ALGERIA

LIBYA

EGYPT

KUWAIT

Persian
Gulf

Oman

Arabian Sea

INDIA

TAIWAN

South China
Sea

Philippine Sea

MAURITANIA

MALI

NIGER

CHAD

SAUDI ARABIA

YEMEN

OMAN

Red
Sea

BANGLADESH

MYANMAR

VIETNAM

PHILIPPINES

GUAM

SUDAN

Gulf of Aden

Bay of Bengal

THAILAND

Andaman
Sea

Gulf of
Thailand

NIGERIA

GUINEA

BURKINA

IVORY
COAST

CENTRAL AFRICAN
REPUBLIC

DJIBOUTI

SOMALIA

SRI LANKA

BRUNEI

PALAU

LIBERIA

EQUATORIAL GUINEA
SAO TOME & PRINCIPE

CAMEROON

ETHIOPIA

MALAYSIA

TANZANIA

KENYA

Indian Ocean

Java Sea

Arafura Sea

PAPUA
NEW GUINEA

COMOROS

Timor Sea

Gulf of
Carpentaria

ANGOLA

ZAMBIA

MALAWI

MADAGASCAR

NAMIBIA

BOTSWANA

ZIMBABWE

MOZAMBIQUE

AUSTRALIA

antic Ocean

SOUTH AFRICA

SWAZILAND

LESOTHO

Great Australian Bight

COORDINATES **41 00 N, 74 00 E**

5

357 SECTION A GRID 3C | 195 SECTION B GRID 3D | 363 SECTION L GRID 4S | 143 SECTION GRID D 49 | 164 SECTION S GRID 4B | 190 SECTION A GRID 3A | 112 SECTION S GRID 3H

SAT-TBlitz22 SIGNAL ANALYSIS
POS 581 31.755-8501 01.761

HAWK

Name: ★ Clayton Abernathy
Call Sign: ★ Hawk
Rank: ★ General
Nationality: ★ American
Specialization: ★ Command
Current Assignment: ★ Commanding Officer, G.I. JOE
Previous Assignment: ★ NATO Forward Command, Afghanistan
Observations of Note: ★ "I've made a career of showing up where I'm needed, whether ordered to or not."

General Clayton 'Hawk' Abernathy was selected as commander of the G.I. JOE unit due to his years of exemplary service in the United States Armed Forces. His leadership style also inspires unwavering loyalty in those under his command.

This highly decorated military officer has a steadfast appreciation for the rules of engagement, tempered by an awareness of the shades of gray involved in dealing with terrorist threats, which results in a tendency to go "off the grid" on occasion to achieve his goals. He is also aware of the necessity for governments to sometimes have plausible deniability.

▶ **PSYCHOLOGICAL PROFILE**

Dennis Quaid (Hawk): General 'Hawk' Abernathy is the leader of the JOEs. I'm the guy who gets to tell everybody what to do. I get to wear the big watch and do all the easy stuff.... We're super soldiers. International soldiers of the future. Special ops, with the thought being that the world could actually come together and cooperate and pool their military intelligence resources and have an organization like G.I. JOE to fight evil organizations, which may crop up here and there.

N.A.T.O.

Designation: ★ North Atlantic Treaty
Organization (NATO)
Description: ★ Military alliance of democratic
states in Europe and North
America
Head of Organization: ★ Secretary General
Current G.I. JOE Liaison: ★ President of the United
States of America

★ The North Atlantic Treaty Organization is an
alliance of countries that signed the North Atlantic
Treaty in 1949, agreeing to work together through political and military means to safeguard their nations' free-
doms and security. NATO provides a forum in which the
United States, Canada, and European countries can
consult together on security issues of common concern,
and take joint action in addressing them.

Twenty-three of the twenty-six member countries
have agreed to participate in the G.I. JOE program, con-
tributing the most skilled members of their intelligence
operations and armed forces to the G.I. JOE team.

★

SPOTLIGHT: Larry Hama, the creator of the original
G.I. JOE comic books, is one of the dignitaries in
the briefing scene at the beginning of the film.

President of the United States

Title: ★ President of the United States

Relevant Functions: ★ Direct liaison with G.I. JOE, especially when the unit is operating on American soil. Representative of NATO as the leader of one of its member countries

★ One of the participating nations in the NATO alliance, the United States of America is under the leadership of a President chosen by election every four years to serve no more than two terms. The office of the current American President coordinates with other participating world leaders in the G.I. JOE program on decisions that jointly affect the team. When a consensus is reached—such as the decision (later rescinded) to disband the G.I. JOE unit—the President relays that information to General Hawk, the American officer currently serving as commander of G.I. JOE.

▶ **PSYCHOLOGICAL PROFILE**

Jonathan Pryce (President): The idea of getting to play the President of the United States has an enormous appeal. I've played lots of powerful figures in the past, but none quite as powerful as this.... In Britain, we have always been aware of the strength of the American President, and how they behave, and how they walk. There's this kind of consistency to it. There's a very proud way that the President walks.

COVER GIRL

Name: ★ Courtney Krieger
Call Sign: ★ Cover Girl
Rank: ★ Corporal
Nationality: ★ Czech
Specialization: ★ Counterintelligence
Previous Assignment: ★ Czech Republic Military Intelligence

Former model turned intelligence operative Courtney 'Cover Girl' Krieger serves as General Hawk's right-hand-person, keeping track of all organizational details related to the G.I. JOE unit. A seasoned diplomat, Cover Girl is part of the public face of the G.I. JOE team, accompanying Hawk on all political missions while maintaining a cover identity separate from the black ops unit. Though her duties fall largely into the administrative category, she is nevertheless a highly trained military operative, able to hold her own in the most intense situations.

▶ PSYCHOLOGICAL PROFILE

Karolina Kurkova (Cover Girl): She is a tough, intelligent woman, who is in counterintelligence. Cover Girl has a lot of experience in dealing with criminal activity, and she keeps the G.I. JOE team informed and updated. She is a tough woman who does not always show her physical strength. She definitely has an inner strength that you can see in her eyes. Cover Girl is always very composed. She never gives much away.

Technology ◢◢◢

SMART TABLET

This ultra-modern "clipboard" is a complete handheld, high-speed computer that allows its authorized user to call up information ranging from basic emails to highly classified documents with a touch of the stylus.

DEFEND CONVOY

Objective: ★ **Weapons transport**
Location: ★ **Kyrgyzstan**
Team Assigned: ★ **NATO American Special Forces unit**
Voluntary Support: ★ **G.I. JOE Team Alpha**
Hostile: ★ **Unidentified**
Status: ★ **Concluded**

A NATO American Special Forces convoy under the leadership of Captain Conrad 'Duke' Hauser was assigned to transport a shipment of prototype warheads from the MARS Industries factory in Kyrgyzstan. The convoy, consisting of Panther patrol vehicles and a Rhino armored truck, with helicopter air support, came under attack from an unidentified enemy with superior firepower.

The enemy force, armed with pulse weaponry, quickly overwhelmed the outmatched NATO unit. G.I. JOE Team Alpha arrived at the scene to support the NATO operatives, using their special skills sets to take on the enemy operatives and defend against the theft of the warheads.

Panther

Model: Patrol vehicle
Code Name: Panther
Engine: 8 cylinder 4 liter

DESIGN CONCEPT

★ **MACHINE GUNS:** Roof-mounted dual machine guns are controlled remotely by soldiers stationed in the rear compartment.

★ **WINDOWS:** Toughened glass composed of automotive glass mixed with bullet resistant optical plastic.

★ The Panther patrol vehicle primarily serves on reconnaissance details and takes point on convoy missions. It is the eyes and ears of any unit.

Attack Helicopter

Model: Attack helicopter
Engine: Twin turboshaft engines

★ The attack helicopter is a twin-engine, advanced aircraft used for reconnaissance, solo attack missions, and providing air support for ground troops. The vehicle is designed to survive a heavy barrage while inflicting maximum damage.

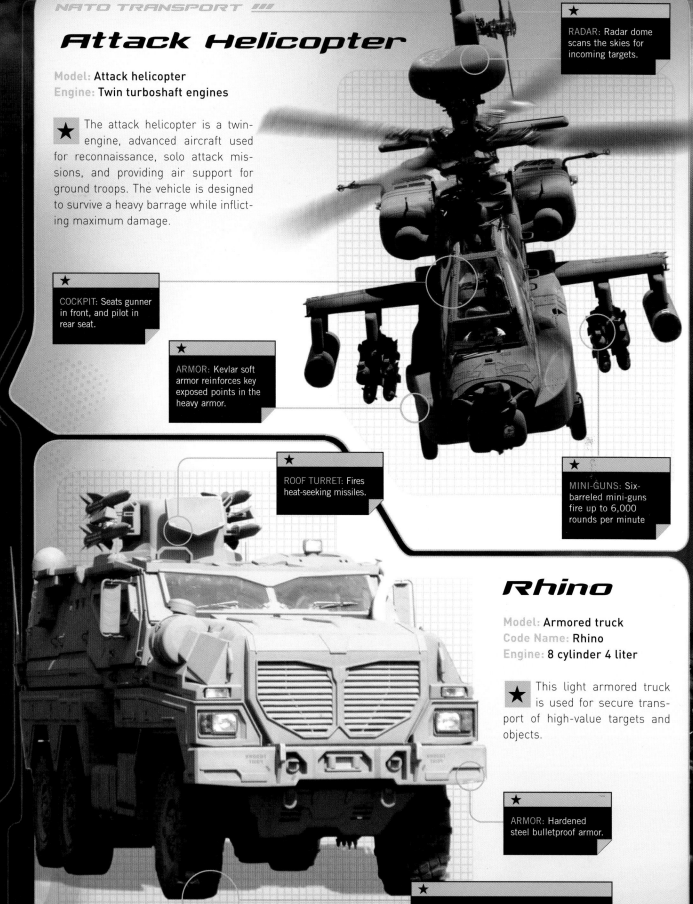

★ RADAR: Radar dome scans the skies for incoming targets.

★ COCKPIT: Seats gunner in front, and pilot in rear seat.

★ ARMOR: Kevlar soft armor reinforces key exposed points in the heavy armor.

★ ROOF TURRET: Fires heat-seeking missiles.

★ MINI-GUNS: Six-barreled mini-guns fire up to 6,000 rounds per minute

Rhino

Model: Armored truck
Code Name: Rhino
Engine: 8 cylinder 4 liter

★ This light armored truck is used for secure transport of high-value targets and objects.

★ ARMOR: Hardened steel bulletproof armor.

★ TIRES: Constructed with a hard plastic liner that enables the vehicle to run for several miles on a flat.

▶ MISSION ANALYSIS

Ed Verreaux (production designer): We had to have a location that we could basically own, that we could control. It really couldn't be any kind of a highway or any place that actually had real traffic on it because there's just no way that we could own it for the several weeks that we were going to be out there shooting. Finally, we went to a movie facility called Big Sky Ranch. It's actually a working ranch out in Simi Valley, and we built a part of the highway out there.... We drove around it quite a bit with Stephen [Sommers], and he finally found a place that he really liked and he said, "Can we put a road here?" I said, "Sure. We'll build a road here." So we built about 400 yards of road.

Greg Michael (second unit director): This is one of these things where it's just a marvel of our special effects. We've got these vehicles that are supposed to be hit by a new breed of weapon, which is the pulse weapon. We've got these huge, ten-ton army trucks and tanks that are literally being crushed and thrown by a pulse weapon. It's like this pressurized air that can basically take a helicopter or even an army tank and crush it like a beer can in an instant. [Special effects coordinator] Dan Sudick and his team took these real vehicles and were able to crush them, toss them and throw them. We had explosions. We had these things flying and flipping through the air, getting crushed like beer cans. It was just an intense, intense sequence.

Ray Park (Snake-Eyes): Snake-Eyes' entrance was, and is, very important to me. The way it was written, it was just key. He was just phenomenal. So in my mind I wanted something great.... I wanted it to be iconic. I wanted it to be really cool. Stephen had said to me he wanted it in one shot, so that really impressed me. I wanted to show the audience that there wasn't any trickery, apart from the wirework. I mean, I had to be on a wire. But I wanted to show that I can do this and so it was really important and I was pumped up. To be above the trees at three in the morning, to land, to take out guys that were six-foot-six intimidating Vipers was really exciting for me. I wanted that to be the time when the audience and the fans go, "There's Snake-Eyes!"

R.A. Rondell (stunt coordinator): Ray Park did a twelve-move entrance that was amazing. The stunt people, we all just sat there in awe that he could remember and nail each move. To be able to come in upside down, flip, land on the ground, draw the sword, take out three guys, pull his pistol, not look, fire, kill two guys here and then hit a posture all in one move.... When they yelled, "Cut," everybody was silent. We were just staring at him like, "Oh my God. How'd he pull that off?" And he did it time after time after time. It was perfect. It was brilliant!

Erik Howsam (executive producer): My big "Geek Moment" is Snake-Eyes' basically bungee jumping out of the airplane at the beginning in the convoy attack. I don't think you could come up with a better, cooler introduction to Snake-Eyes if you tried. For me, when I first heard that idea that Stuart Beattie had, I went crazy. I couldn't wait to see that filmed. I think in the movie it comes off great.

I would say the whole Snake-Eyes storyline and his battle with Storm Shadow, those are my geekiest moments by far. I just love that aspect of it. That's the character that I loved growing up. That's the one that I would sit there and draw and sketch as I was watching the cartoon. When I grew up in the early eighties, ninjas were huge. And here comes a property called G.I. JOE where you have a ninja commando. There's nothing cooler than that.

DESTRO

Name: ★ James McCullen
Alias: ★ Destro
Current Position: ★ Founder & CEO of MARS Industries
Nationality: ★ Scottish
Specialization: ★ Heavy weapons
Profession: ★ Arms developer and dealer

James McCullen, CEO of MARS Industries, prefers to think of himself as an "armament solutions engineer" rather than using the undignified term "arms dealer."

No matter what title he answers to, McCullen is clearly at the forefront of the global weapons trade. Following in the footsteps of his ancestors, the industrialist has taken the family business and grown it into one of the most successful enterprises in the world. His personal philosophy that the world is in need of unification has always appeared to be a noble sentiment, though recent actions he has taken to achieve this goal undermine that impression.

It has been reported that McCullen was badly burned during the recent engagement with the G.I. JOE unit and his appearance may have been altered.

FLAME THROWER

These compact, portable models emit jets of flame that can travel over several meters.

McCullen Family: James McCullen's ancestral namesake was held in the Bastille Prison in 1641 after being found guilty of treason for selling military arms to the enemy of King Louis XIII while, at the same time, providing weapons to His Royal Highness.

★ History records that the first James McCullen's personal philosophy held that it was the McCullen destiny "to run the wars, not simply to supply arms." The French called him "Destro: Destroyer of Nations."

In place of a death sentence, a metal mask was forged to fit the prisoner so that he could serve as an example and that "no man, woman, nor child may ever see [his] treacherous face for the rest of [his] natural life." McCullen wore that metal prison until the day of his death.

It is believed the mask is currently in the possession of his descendant, where it is rumoured to serve as a symbol of the vendetta that the McCullen family continues to hold against the French government to this day.

MEDALLION: Destro is rarely seen without this McCullen family heirloom, which he has had reset as a tie-pin.

DESTRO'S MASK

Brad Einhorn (property master): We really tried to reference Destro's mask [from the comic books] so people know it when they see it. I think I have accomplished that, because when people do see the mask, the first thing they say is, "Destro." We worked from research into masks from the time period, but then we gave it a full face—the silver face—so it looks like Destro.

Stephen Sommers (director): The main villain, if he has this kind of technology, weaponry, and facilities at his disposal, he would have to be an extremely rich individual. It would take generations to become a guy like Destro. You can't just do this overnight. It's the rare person—Bill Gates—who creates an empire from scratch that's worth that kind of money.

So we introduce his ancestor and we see that Clan McCullen was dealing arms hundreds of years ago. It also sets up the Destro mask. You look at a character and you go, "Okay, this guy has a metal mask.... Why is he wearing this metal mask?" You can't just start a movie and have a guy walking around wearing a metal mask and not explain it to the ninety percent of the audience that doesn't know G.I. JOE inside and out. We used as much as we could out of the comic books and the mythology of the cartoon, but then we had to make up some of our own.

VIPER

ARMOR: Custom-made body armor and helmet make Viper's immediately recognisable.

 It was recently discovered that MARS Industries employs hundreds of freelance soldiers as James McCullen's personal army. These fully expendable Viper troops have a wide variety of skills sets depending on where they are needed to function within the organization. Vipers are clad head to toe in bulletproof battle armor that can withstand blasts from an assault rifle. Their generic helmets serve the dual purpose of hiding their identity and as a reminder that, no matter what role they serve, they are each anonymous grunts in their leader's eyes.

Development art designs for the Viper helmet.

Weaponry ///

PULSE RIFLE

Cutting-edge weapons technology. More powerful than the pistol, the energy pulse from these rifles can crush metal and punch through a vehicle's armor plating. Accessories include a night-vision scope and laser sight.

DESIGN CONCEPT

ZARTAN

Name: ★ Unknown
Alias: ★ Zartan
Current Position: ★ Unkown
Previous Position: ★ Aide-de-camp to
James McCullen
Nationality: ★ Unknown
Specialization: ★ Heavy weapons
Profession: ★ Mercenary.
Master of disguise

::: ALERT! :::

In light of his access to MARS Industries' technology, including the possible applications for nano-mites, it is likely that any recent changes to his appearance are extensive and convincingly accurate. His current location is unknown. Identification of his target is a priority.

Little is known about this individual, who was first seen by G.I. JOE operatives as McCullen's aide-de-camp, although Cover Girl made note that the mysterious man seemed to possess a natural ability to mimic those around him. Further investigation has revealed that he is a mercenary known to be a master of disguise.

Intel suggests that Zartan is so committed to his work as a chameleonic mimic that he will spend upwards of a year studying a particular subject. Infinity Scans of recent (rare) surveillance photographs of the operative have revealed that he has lost forty percent of his muscle mass in the past eighteen months. It is conjectured that he may be preparing to replace a specific, unidentified individual.

▶ **PSYCHOLOGICAL PROFILE**
Arnold Vosloo (Zartan): I get to wear different things. I get to wear a suit in this movie, I get to wear combat fatigues, I get to be a camel herder at one point, because Zartan's a master of disguise. He assumes these different identities throughout the film.... He's a mercenary who hires himself out to Destro. In the comic book series he would hire himself out to anybody, in fact. The highest bidder. Pure mercenary. A little like an actor, I suppose!

FINGERPRINT REMOVER: This device permanently removes the subjects fingerprints using cutting-edge laser technology.

EGYPT

0°   30°   60°   90°   120°   15

Greenland Sea

Norwegian Sea

RUSSIA

Sea of Okhot

SWEDEN
FINLAND
Gulf of Bothnia
North Sea
DENMARK
Baltic Sea
IRELAND   U.K.   NETH.
GERMANY
English Channel   LUX.   POLAND   BYELARUS
CZECH
Bay of Biscay   FRANCE   ITALY   Black Sea   UKRAINE   KAZAKHSTAN   MONGOLIA   NORTH KOREA   Sea of Japan
PORTUGAL   SPAIN   TURKEY   GEORGIA   SOUTH KOREA
Mediterranean Sea   Caspian   THE PIT DEFENCE   JAPAN
26°50'01N 30°44'16E   CHINA   East China Sea
MOROCCO   ACCESS FILE   North Pa
ALGERIA   EGYPT   IRAN   AFGHANISTAN   TAIWAN
y Islands
MAURITANIA   LIBYA   SAUDI ARABIA   Gulf of Oman   MYANMAR   South China Sea   Philippine Sea   GUAM
MALI   NIGER   CHAD   Red Sea   YEMEN   OMAN   Arabian Sea   INDIA   Bay of Bengal   LAOS   VIETNAM   PHILIPPINES   PALAU
BURKINA   SUDAN   Gulf of Aden   Andaman   Gulf of   BRUNEI
GUINEA   NIGERIA   SRI LANKA   Sea   Thailand   MALAYSIA
SIERRA LEONE   IVORY COAST   CENTRAL AFRICAN   ETHIOPIA
LIBERIA   EQUATORIAL GUINEA   KENYA   Java Sea   PAPUA NEW GUINEA
SAO TOME & PRINCIPE   ZAIRE   BURU   TANZANIA   Arafura Sea
Indian Ocean   Timor Sea   Gulf of Carpentaria
COMOROS
ANGOLA   ZAMBIA   MALAWI
NAMIBIA   BOTSWANA   MOZAMBIQUE   MADAGASCAR   AUSTRALIA
SWAZILAND
antic Ocean   SOUTH AFRICA   LESOTHO   Great Australian Bight

COORDINATES 27 00 N, 30 00 E

5

357 SECTION A GRID 2C   195 SECTION B GRID 3D   263 SECTION L GRID 45   143 SECTION 6 GRID D 49   164 SECTION 5 GRID 48   190 SECTION A GRID 2A   113 SECTION 5 GRID 3H

SAT-TBlitz22   SIGNAL ANALYSIS
POS   581 31.755-8501 01.761

G.I. JOE

Designation: G.I. JOE
Current Commander:
 General Clayton
 'Hawk' Abernathy
Motto: "Knowing is
 half the battle."

★ G.I. JOE is an ultra-black ops (highly secret covert operations) special forces unit comprised of the top men and women from the finest military organizations in the world. "JOE" team members are chosen for their specialized skills as well as their ability to perform across all levels of engagement. They do not require mission specific training—they can handle any situation, no matter how extreme.

G.I. JOE was formed when the nations of the world determined that a joint task force was required to deal with the rising terrorist threat to the global community. Initially, ten nations signed up, quickly increasing to the current number of twenty-three.

▶ TEAM ANALYSIS
Lorenzo di Bonaventura (producer): What brings them together is that they're the best of the best. They're sent on these incredible missions against these incredible bad guys. Each one has a particular thing that they're really good at, and the team counts on the fact that they can do that. Together, the individual parts of it make more than the whole.

Stuart Beattie (screenplay writer): I think what makes G.I. JOE different from all the regular comic book series is it really is a cast of characters rather than just focusing on one person and their demons. It really is a group of people and how they band together to get the job done.

Stephen Sommers (director): After 9/11 and what's been going on in the last few years, my attitude is if there isn't an outfit like G.I. JOE, there sure should be. It's very obvious to everybody that we need a global unit that's special forces. That can go anywhere at any time. I just thought G.I. JOE was that kind of outfit. They are special forces. They don't fight wars, they fight the battles.... We not only need the best of the best from America, we need the best of the best from all of our allies around the world.

Lieutenant Colonel Paul Sinor (U.S. Army Liaison): When a production company comes to the Army requesting support for a TV show or a feature film, it comes to my office. We have three very strict guidelines that we go by, but they're kind of loose in how we interpret them. That sounds like a dichotomy, but we look for A) real soldiers doing real things; what a real soldier would do in his or her normal duty. B) We look for them doing it in a realistic manner, within the parameters of the film. In other words, if it's a science fiction film and they're fighting monsters, well, we don't fight monsters, but if we did, is that how we would do it? And C) it has to have some positive image with regard to public relations, public information, something like that.

G.I. JOE is an American icon. It would be very difficult for us not to be able to support that, just from the name alone. G.I. JOE today is not what G.I. JOE was twenty or thirty years ago when many people first met G.I. JOE and started playing with the toy. G.I. JOE has been a part of American history for the last forty years and we're delighted to be a part of it.

Howler

Model: Jet
Code Name: Howler

DESIGN CONCEPT ///

★ WEAPONRY: Armed with heat-seeking missiles.

★ THRUSTERS: Four winged jet thrusters rotate ninety degrees for vertical takeoff and landing. Left and right thrusters function independently for evasive maneuvers.

★ The next generation Jet provides troop transport for G.I. JOE strike teams of up to a dozen soldiers. Thrust vectoring allows for vertical/short takeoff and landing, combining the convenience of fixed-winged flight at supersonic speeds in excess of Mach 3 with the practicality of helicopter style maneuvering.

TRANSPORT ///

Spyder

Model: Attack vehicle
Code Name: Spyder

★ The Spyder attack vehicle is an armored, high-speed, all-terrain cycle that boasts a considerable selection of defensive weaponry. Its tri-wheeled design allows for easy handling and maneuverability in the most extreme environments.

BASE OF OPERATIONS

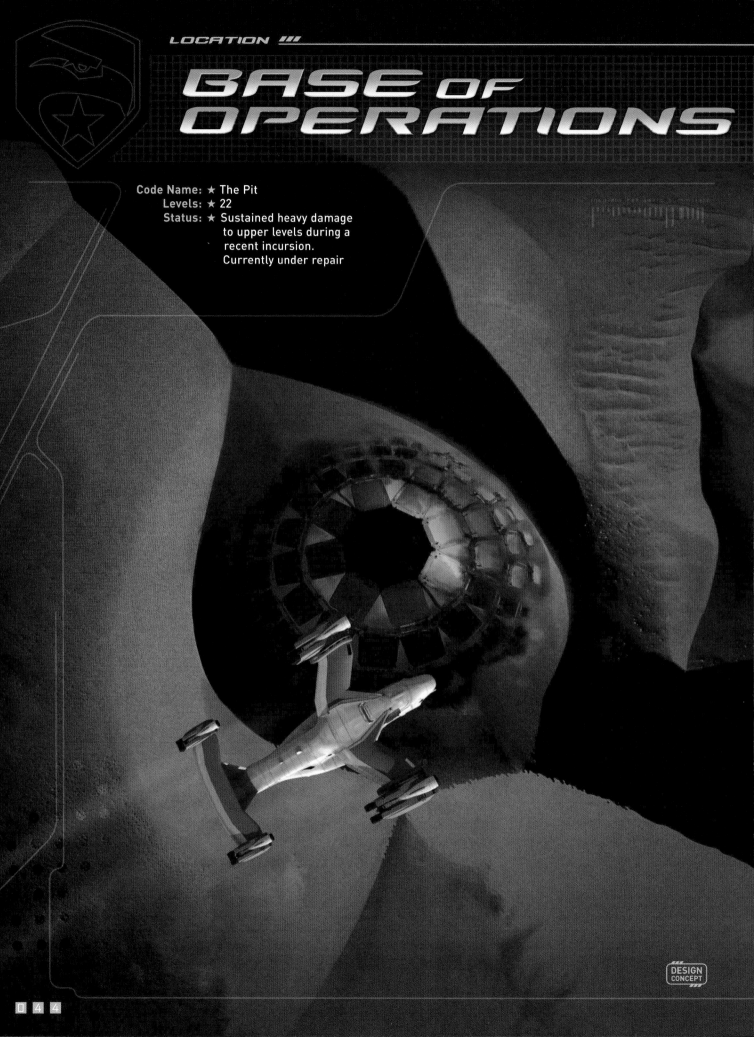

Code Name: ★ The Pit
Levels: ★ 22
Status: ★ Sustained heavy damage
to upper levels during a
recent incursion.
Currently under repair

DESIGN
CONCEPT

The G.I. JOE Tactical Operations Center, known informally as "The Pit," lies at an undisclosed location. Built twenty-two levels deep, this command center serves as a training, housing, research, and communications base for the unit. A fully-contained underground city, The Pit provides for all of the G.I. JOE team needs, from medical to culinary to recreational. The most impressive feature of The Pit is the various training levels set up to recreate a multitude of battle environments, including the Deep Sea Combat Level, Arctic Combat Level, and Urban Combat Level.

The location of the main entrance to The Pit is highly classified. The process of opening the main entrance requires the displacement of several tons of sand to reveal a landing platform capable of handling aircraft and surface vehicles. The platform descends into The Pit, with a section that continues on as an elevator for personnel transport dropping deeper into the facility. Each level serves a different function from command to training facilities to the barracks for G.I. JOE team members.

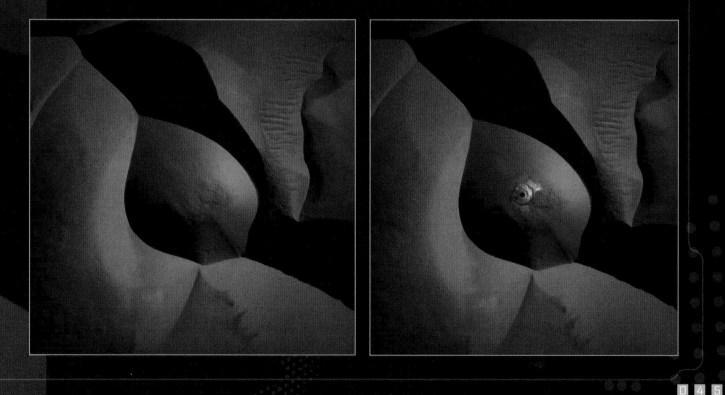

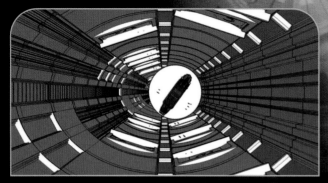

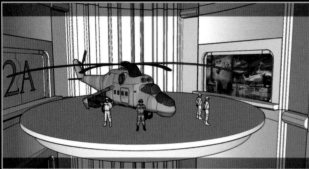

★

ELEVATOR: A massive platform that descends from the entrance to the hangar level of The Pit, where the G.I. JOE vehicles are housed and maintained.

DESIGN ANALYSIS

Lorenzo di Bonaventura (producer): I've been involved in a lot of big movies. This is one of the biggest movies I've ever seen. The scale of this movie is enormous. The architecture of it is very specific. It has to be extremely, exceedingly specific because you have to create three worlds: the world of the good guys, where their private world is; the world of the bad guys, their private world; and then the world that we're all living in. It's really demanding on Stephen Sommers, to give us real specificity about how to differentiate where we're at all times.

Ed Verreaux (production designer): We would do illustrations, and then I'd show them to Stephen. Then he'd say, "Yeah, what about this?" and "What about that?" and "I was thinking that there ought to be this." So we went through about three different design iterations until we sort of came upon the one that is ultimately going to be in the movie.

From that point, we began to design the actual set pieces so that would reflect the overall design. Now, of course, we don't really build the entire Urban Combat Level. We've built the set, and it only goes up forty feet. But the Urban Combat Level's a whole lot bigger than that. The rest of it will be extended with visual effects set extensions, so there'll be these incredibly huge spaces that you'll see. And it's all part of the Urban Combat Level.

DESIGN CONCEPT

Kate Sullivan (set decorator): It was really a collaborative effort between the art department, construction, stunts, and special effects. We often had to create multiples for explosions and stunt effects. In some of the fight sequences we had to provide special furniture to aid the stunt performers, as well as creating break-aways [sets with elements, such as walls, that can be removed to accommodate filming equipment]. In several of the sets we had to provide dressing that was completely expendable because of the fire, explosion and crash stunts involved.

Control Room

★ The control room is the communications center of The Pit, providing the main link to the outside world. Security officers staff the room at all times, controlling access to the facility and manning the early warning systems ready to sound the alert at the first sign of attack. Cameras equipped with infrared, night vision, and X-ray scanning are stationed in secured locations above ground to monitor the vicinity while radar scans the skies above and earthquake sensors monitor seismic activity in the area. Computer stations can link with satellite surveillance to keep an eye on hot spots all over the globe.

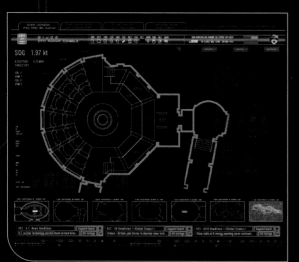

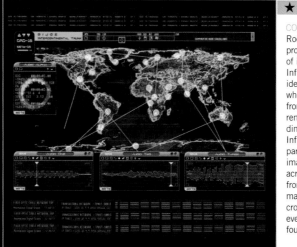

★ COMPUTERS: Control Room computers can process a massive amount of information through an Infinity Scan. Subject identification is achieved when an image pulled from a video camera is rendered into a three-dimensional likeness. The Infinity Scan then compares that rendering to images taken from servers across the globe—whether from cameras at ATM machines, airports, or crowd shots at sporting events—until a match is found.

3D HOLO-PROJECTOR

The holographic projector is a communications device that casts a lifelike image of a subject from a separate location. A series of holographic cameras built along the walls of a room capture 360 degree views of a subject that are transmitted to a holo-projector processor that merges those images into a life-sized three-dimensional projection. The holo-projector comes in both wall-mounted and portable versions.

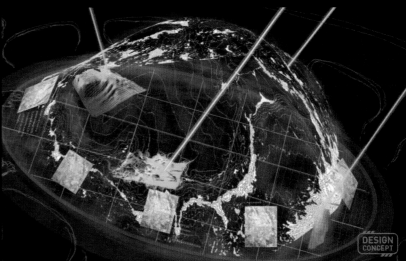

DESIGN CONCEPT

DESIGN CONCEPT

Recreation Room

KNOWING IS HALF THE BATTLE

★ JOEs can kick back and relax in a rec room that includes a full gym equipped with free weights, punching bags, and exercise machines. They can also exercise their minds with areas sectioned off for meditation (with or without swords) or a game of chess.

▶ DESIGN ANALYSIS

Kate Sullivan (set decorator): In the Rec Room, Hasbro wanted to include several items that the fans would recognize as being part of the world of G.I. JOE. They were called "Easter Eggs." As in, "How many eggs are hidden in the following scene?" They included a Yo JOE Cola vending machine, dog bowls for Snake-Eyes' pet wolf, Timber, and "Knowing is half the Battle" painted on the wall. We also added such things as Bazooka's jersey framed on the wall, vintage G.I. JOE dolls selectively placed around the set, and a pair of white ski poles and a white jacket suggesting that Snow-Job is somewhere in the vicinity, although we don't get to see him in this version.

Combat Levels

★ One of several massive training facilities designed to prepare JOEs for engagement in a variety of terrain, the Urban Combat Level recreates conditions typical to populated cities. It includes the "Terrorist Course," an exam that tests a participant's ability to take down twenty terrorists in sixty seconds. The record for dispatching all twenty terrorists is held by Scarlett.

A general combat training area is equipped for a variety of hand-to-hand battle scenarios. Electrified pugil sticks provide added incentive for success in this arena.

Emergency munitions are stationed throughout this level for use in training.

A United States Army serviceman for the past decade, Conrad 'Duke' Hauser was leading an elite NATO sanctioned American Special Forces unit when he first engaged the G.I. JOE unit. This was not the first time the special unit had crossed paths with the captain. Duke had previously been considered for membership in G.I. JOE four years earlier. One of General Hawk's subordinates attempted to recruit the officer while in Thailand. It was determined that his emotional state at the time, following a substantial mission failure, made him an unsuitable candidate for inclusion in the team.

During the current crisis, Duke used his intimate knowledge of an enemy agent to convince General Hawk that he would be a valuable addition to the team. Duke scored in the top half-percent of all the people ever tested in the Urban Combat Level training facility at G.I. JOE headquarters and was offered a position in the organization once he passed muster in the field.

INJURY: Battle scar under right eye incurred during a classified mission.

DESIGN CONCEPT

Super suit and equipment vest original concept design.

▶ PSYCHOLOGICAL PROFILE

Channing Tatum (Duke): He'll die for his friends. He'll run straight into gunfire without thinking. That's what I see Duke as. He's just no-holds-barred. He knows he's got to get the mission done and he's got to protect his men and he'll do anything that it takes to do that....

It's a pretty strange, surreal thing to have a little action figure that you played with and now you're sort of supposed to be him. It's a little weird.

★ weaponry ///

★

HK416 ASSAULT RIFLE: NATO issued
assault weapon that fires up to 900 rounds
per minute.

RIPCORD

Name: ★ Wallace Weems
Call Sign: ★ Ripcord
Rank: ★ Lieutenant
Nationality: ★ American
Specialization: ★ Marksmanship. Pilot (jet qualified)
Current Assignment: ★ G.I. JOE Team Alpha
Previous Assignment: ★ NATO American Special
Forces Unit, Kyrgyzstan
Observations of Note: ★ "I didn't 'steal' that Blackhawk,
I was borrowing it...."

Wallace 'Ripcord' Weems has spent a decade serving in the U.S. Armed Forces, often in the position of second-in-command to Conrad 'Duke' Hauser. Flying since he was thirteen years old, Ripcord logs time in the air on every leave to keep his piloting qualification up to date. In addition to piloting skills, Ripcord is a weapons specialist and an expert marksman, considered the second best in his battalion. Shortly before being accepted into the G.I. JOE unit, he had requested an application to the U.S. Air Force.

Known to be a bit of a joker—and a lover as much as a fighter—Ripcord never allows his laid back attitude to impact his responsibilities in the field. Neither the blemish on his record for the time he "borrowed" a Blackhawk helicopter, nor achieving a slightly lower score that Duke in the Urban Combat Level test prevented him from being accepted into the G.I. JOE team.

Marlon Wayans (Ripcord): Duke likes to fight. Hence the scar under his eye. Ripcord doesn't like to. He knows how to, but he'd prefer to fly. Duke wants to be in the battle. I prefer to fly over the battle. I want to go to Air Force. I'm not even thinking about G.I. JOE.... Everybody in this movie is a bad ass to some extent. I'm probably the least bad ass of them all, until I get in that plane. Then I'm a bad ass.

Liquid Armor

Model: Liquid armor
Function: Protection

⭐ The flexible, full body armor is created using a mixture of hard nanoparticles and non-evaporating liquid that molds to the body. Liquid armor suits are resistant to puncture while not restricting range of movement. This modern day version of chainmail is practically impenetrable, protecting the wearer from a variety of projectiles.

▶ DESIGN ANALYSIS

Ellen Mirojnick (costume designer): How other superhero movies work is that you build an inner structure, a muscle suit, underneath the garment, so that the superhero will look super. The body will be enhanced and be fabulous, no matter what. We didn't want to do that. Basically, I designed a suit of liquid armor that is a muscle suit worn on the outside of their bodies, so that you see the musculature and the anatomy on the outside.

Liquid armor really is a product. It's used in high-performance ski-wear, a lot of athletic things, the army, et cetera, so that when you hit the ground, it's a protecting force. It's usually inside a garment. You will never see what it looks like.

DEFEND THE PIT

Objective: ★ Defend G.I. JOE headquarters
Location: ★ The Pit
Team Assigned: ★ All G.I. JOE teams
Hostile: ★ Possible identification as forces under the command of James McCullen
Status: ★ Concluded

Enemy agents attacked G.I. JOE headquarters, The Pit, after determining the classified location via subterfuge. Under the command of Baroness DeCobray, the invading force consisted of operatives identified as Zartan, Storm Shadow, and several foot soldiers known under the uniform title "Neo-Vipers." Their initial entrance into the facility went undetected until a member of the JOE unit engaged with the trespassers and activated the intruder alert. At which point all G.I. JOE team members on the premises took up defensive stations and engaged the enemy using all available weaponry at their disposal.

► MISSION ANALYSIS
Cliff Lanning (first assistant director): It's part superhero film, part ninja film, part spy film. There are goodies and baddies. Good and evil. Huge, wide scope environments: one moment you are at the bottom of the sea; next you're at the top of the stratosphere; you're on land; you're in the desert. You're all over the place. If you could write a script and say, "Put in 'scope,'" that's what this film's got.

Rachel Nichols (Scarlett): We really trained, Sienna Miller and myself. The boys are all really jealous because they fire a lot of weapons and they get to set off a lot of bombs and fly airplanes and everything, but Sienna and I get the best fight in the movie, I'd say. Well, the Storm Shadow-Snake-Eyes fight is pretty rad as well....

Sienna and I trained five days a week, about two hours a day for about six weeks before we started shooting. We learned a ninety-move fight sequence, which is the big elevator fight.

A fight scene is so much fun to shoot because after you complete it, you think, "If a guy tries to mug me in a dark alley, I can totally take him out." Which may or may not be true, but we definitely trained extremely hard for it. So I hope it shows!

Sienna Miller (the Baroness): There was one moment when we were filming where [Rachel] kicked and it went to the wrong place, and I responded naturally and blocked it. It was just this moment of, "Wow, something's clicked." It became instinctual, which I never thought would happen.

When I turned up, I was like, "There is no way I'm going to be able to do this." But actually, by the end, I was loving it. I think it'll be a pretty good girl fight.

R.A. Rondell (stunt coordinator): We started boxing and throwing a few punches and kicks, and the style developed immediately with them. For Rachel, it was because her stature was tall and she held her hands in a certain way. She was more of a boxer type. She was elongated and she was making moves. With Sienna, being a little bit shorter, it was a little more grounded and she started throwing kicks. And then it immediately clicked. So I sat back and started watching them. It was a perfect blend of Sienna being into a lot more of the kicking action and Rachel being a little taller with the hands, and they just started matching up beautifully. Then we started working with them, and their desire to train really showed. They were in the gym almost every day. They were calling us, saying, "When can we come to the gym? When can we work on these fights? When can we work on this?" It was really special.

Jet Pack

Model: Jet Pack

★ The rocket propelled jet pack is worn on the back for personal air transport. Vector controls direct the winged jet to fly in any direction. Though intended for individual transport, each jet pack is weight-tested to a capacity of two average-sized adults.

DESIGN CONCEPT

★ A pair of jet packs are usually stored, mounted on a wall rack, in the Urban Combat Level.

DESIGN CONCEPT

THE BARONESS

Name: ★ Baroness Anastasia DeCobray
Alias: ★ The Baroness
Profession: ★ Saboteur

Baroness Anastasia DeCobray is the wife of Baron Daniel DeCobray, the noted French scientist heading the research team developing the particle accelerator. The pair makes their home in a chateau in Paris with a view of the Eiffel Tower. It is now believed that the Baroness only entered their marriage to help encourage the scientist in his work with the particle accelerator, a necessary component in the weaponizing process for the nanotech warheads developed by MARS Industries. Her proximity to the man was clearly beneficial in a plan to deploy the technology.

The Baroness is a very different person from the woman who suffered a devastating change of fortune in her personal life four years earlier. In the intervening time, "Ana" admits to joining James McCullen in his plot to upset the global balance of power. A skilled combatant, the Baroness has received intensive fight training from the assassin Storm Shadow.

▶ **PSYCHOLOGICAL PROFILE**
Sienna Miller (the Baroness): She can fight, she can kick, she can fire guns, any sort of weapon. I'm vicious! But I think underneath it all there is this sensitive side.... In amongst all this violence and this chaos, there's this love story going on—this dynamic between these two people that were once very in love and are battling their own demons.

The Baron

★ Baron Daniel DeCobray descends from a long line of influential French aristocrats. A respected physicist, he is the head of a Paris-based classified project to construct a particle accelerator for the French Ministry of Defense, and lives at the DeCobray family seat on the outskirts of the city. The extremely wealthy scientist married the mysterious Anastasia after a whirlwind courtship and is evidently deeply in love with his wife.

▶ **DESIGN ANALYSIS**

Sienna Miller (the Baroness): I get the best gadgets. I've got glasses that if I touch the stem they turn from clear to dark!

Ellen Mirojnick (costume designer): Sienna's just the most fabulous girl-next-door and she had to be turned into the Baroness. We did it with magic and she was all up for it. She said, "Come and paint the Baroness on me." And so we did. We just carved her out and sculpted her. We made her have a little bit of a couture edge because Sienna could carry that off. We added some, I would say, "fashionable" elements to her gear. That's what I basically did throughout. I would say that it came from not only the comic world but a bit of a fashion base as well.

★

COSTUME: A special chair, or "leaning board," was constructed for Sienna Miller because she lacked flexibility in her form-fitting body armor and could not rest in an actual seat once she was in costume.

★

PULSE PISTOL:
Fires an energy pulse capable of crushing a human body.

★

GLASSES: Form follows function with these spectacles that become sunglasses with a touch of the stem. The lenses also contain a heads-up display and can zoom in on and scan objects for analysis.

SCANNER

Emits scanning beams in a 360 degree arc which detect and record structural details and human movement, creating a 3D schematic of a building and its occupants' movements.

Mole Pod

Model: Tunneling vehicle
Code Name: Mole Pod

DESIGN CONCEPT

★ The single-person tunneling vehicle uses a massive drill bit to burrow through earth and rock. Each unit has a self-contained oxygen and climate control system. The driver sits in a supine position in the reinforced glass and steel capsule that makes up the body of the pod. The extended steering column places the touch screen control monitor within comfortable reach of the vehicle operator. Ground penetrating radar continually updates the operator on progress and potential obstacles.

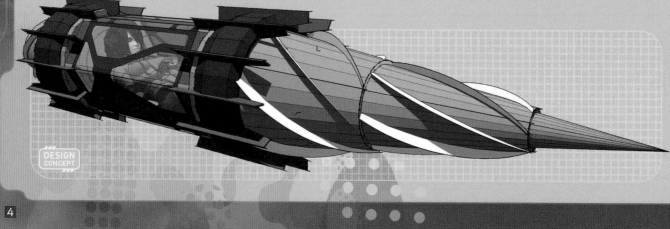

DESIGN CONCEPT

 TRANSPORT ///

Razor

Model: Gunship
Code Name: Razor

★ The Razor gunship is a Jump Jet style aircraft with six jet thrusters capable of vertical takeoff and landing. It is highly armed and armored for the ultimate in battle readiness, employing stealth technology that makes it impossible to register on radar.

★ **CANNONS:** Retractable Concussion Cannons emerge from ports on both sides of the aircraft. The cannons fire subatomic blasts that can crush an armored helicopter.

DESIGN CONCEPT

★ **ARMOR:** Angled armor is lightweight and bulletproof.

HATCH: Side hatch allows for ease of troop loading and off-loading.

MINI-GUN: Fires 6,000 rounds per minute.

DESIGN CONCEPT

TRANSPORTATION SPIKE

A grappling line fired from the Razor's underside has a metal spike that opens to form a foothold for an individual to be lifted into the ship while it is in flight.

NEO-VIPER

Name: Neo-Viper
Current Position: Elite soldier in
MARS Industries' army

★ Twenty mercenaries were selected as test subjects for the painful procedure that turned them into the ultimate super soldiers. The operation is a prime example of twisting beneficial technology for nefarious means. An incision was made behind the right ear of each subject and 1,000 CCs of nano-mite solution was injected into their bodies. These nano-mites attacked the central nervous system, placing the test subjects under the complete control of their leader, and turning them into Neo-Vipers.

It has been suggested that the individual known as the Doctor played a key role in developing the technology used to create the Neo-Vipers.

▶ **PSYCHOLOGICAL PROFILE**
Stuart Beattie (screenplay writer):
You've got all the Vipers, and the Neo-Vipers, which are the foot soldiers that go up against the JOEs. You've got a bunch of these really crazy guys who've all got these nano-mites inside them that are taking away their sense of fear, their sense of pain, and giving them abject loyalty. They'll do anything. They'll go to their deaths without blinking an eye. So you've got this really formidable foe that the JOEs are going up against. Who will win? I can't say....

★ CAMERA: The chestplate of each Neo-Viper is equipped with a button camera that allows McCullen to watch the action from a distant location.

★ PULSE WEAPONS: Neo-Vipers are equipped with both a pulse rifle and pulse pistol.

NEO-VIPER GRENADES

DOCTOR'S PDA: The "destroy" command remotely sets the nano-mites to self-destruct mode, where they literally eat away the body of the Neo-Viper so that he cannot be accessed for information.

Complete inactivity in the self-preservation region of the cortex indicates that Neo-Vipers do not experience fear.

Frontal lobe concepts of morality are disengaged, keeping the soldiers from experiencing remorse.

A complete shut down of the cortical nerve clusters blocks the subject from feeling pain.

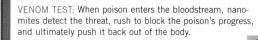

VENOM TEST: When poison enters the bloodstream, nano-mites detect the threat, rush to block the poison's progress, and ultimately push it back out of the body.

FRANCE

ASSAULT ON PARIS
48°52'23N 2°17'47E
ACCESS FILE

PARIS

COORDINATES 48 00 N, 2 00 E

357 SECTION A. GRID 3C | 195 SECTION B GRID 3D | 263 SECTION L GRID 4S | 143 SECTION GRID D 49 | 164 SECTION S GRID 4B | 190 SECTION A GRID 3A | 112 SECTION S GRID 3H

SAT-TBlitz22   SIGNAL ANALYSIS
POS   583 31.755-8501 01-761

HEAVY DUTY

Name: ★ Hershel Dalton
Call Sign: ★ Heavy Duty
Rank: ★ Sergeant
Nationality: ★ British
Specialization: ★ Heavy weapons
Current Assignment: ★ G.I. JOE Team Alpha
Previous Assignment: ★ United Kingdom
Special Forces
Observations of Note: ★ "Yo JOE!"

Hershel 'Heavy Duty' Dalton is an expert in all portable weaponry traditional to infantry troops. He specializes in arms categorized as "heavy weaponry," including, but not limited to: machine guns, grenade launchers, mortars, and anti-tank weapons. Heavy Duty often serves as field commander, coordinating operations between units during engagement, frequently tracking efforts from behind the wheel of an assault vehicle or piloting a submersible SHARC vessel. Heavy Duty also oversees the testing of potential members for the G.I. JOE unit.

weaponry

MINI GUN

Multi-barrel machine gun fires up to 6,000 rounds per minute. The traditionally mounted, eighty pound gun was redesigned with a handheld configuration to allow for personal transport.

Adewale Akinnuoye-Agbaje (Heavy Duty): The most fun I had was shooting my big cannon gun. At 600 rounds per second that was a ride in and of itself. You actually get an adrenalin high. Seeing the envy on my fellow cast-mates' faces made it all the sweeter.

DUAL MACHINE GUN / GRENADE LAUNCHER
Heavy artillery assault weapon combined with the
multi-grenade launcher.

▶ PSYCHOLOGICAL PROFILE

Adewale Akinnuoye-Agbaje: I already had a working relationship with the director, Steve Sommers, from *The Mummy Returns*. I had really enjoyed that experience. He makes shooting big films a lot of fun and really creates an atmosphere where you are going on an adventure. So when he asked me to join him on his next venture I jumped at the chance. Plus it gave me an opportunity, for the first time in my career, to play a character based upon my own accent: British. But besides this I really could not resist the opportunity for me to be a big kid cladding up in funky battle gear and running around with big guns and toys. It's every schoolboy's dream. I am a kid at heart.

★ **ARMOR:** State of the art body armor protects the wearer from small arms fire and the concussion from explosions.

★ **MACHINE PISTOL:** Custom made pistol for rapid firing in close quarters.

★ **UTILITY BELT:** Custom-ised to hold a variety of tools and weapons, including grenades.

DESIGN CONCEPT

BREAKER

Name: ★ Abel Shaz
Call Sign: ★ Breaker
Rank: ★ Corporal
Nationality: ★ Moroccan
Specialization: ★ Communications
Current Assignment: ★ G.I. JOE Team Alpha
Previous Assignment: ★ Royal Moroccan Armed Forces
Observations of Note: ★ "I am the best at this!
Nobody can do what
I just did!"

Abel 'Breaker' Shaz prefers mind games to battle, but he is nevertheless quite adept in a fight. This communications expert is a walking computer, loaded down with the latest in cutting-edge scanning and surveillance technology. The voice of the outfit, Breaker coordinates G.I. JOE team positions during battle, running operation scenarios and providing updates to the units in the field. His light-hearted attitude breaks the tension in the most dire situations, but this skilled chess player knows when the time for seriousness is at hand.

Surveillance Suit

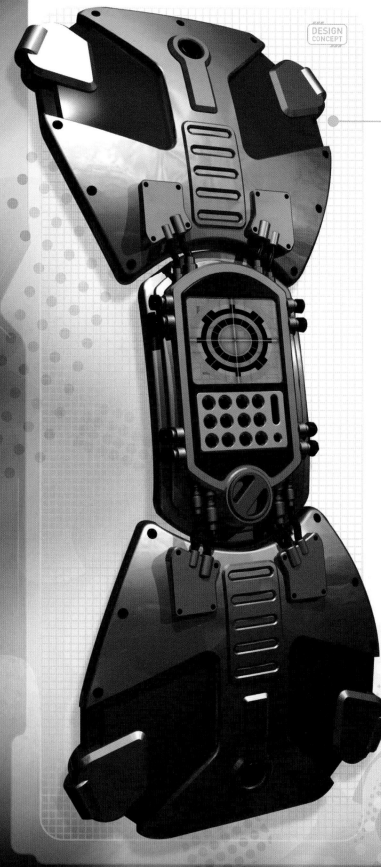

DESIGN CONCEPT

COMPUTER VEST

A wrist-mounted keyboard links to the central processing unit (CPU) in Breaker's computer vest. This portable computer feeds information to the suit monitors, HUD, and 3D holo-projector.

★

VOICE STRESS ANALYZER: Detects changes in speech to determine whether or not a subject is lying.

★

HEADS-UP DISPLAY (HUD): Personalized transparent display that projects information and images called up from Breaker's computer suit. The ball-eye-piece can be set to scan for tracking devices and has multiple viewing options, including zooming features, X-ray, night vision, and infrared.

DESIGN CONCEPT

3D HOLO-PROJECTOR

Projects three-dimensional holographic images from the CPU for analysis.

7.00"

19.34"

DESIGN CONCEPT

Collapsed Carrying Position

Extended Spike and Projector Head

► **PSYCHOLOGICAL PROFILE**

Said Taghmaoui (Breaker): Breaker is the guy who handles the communication for the unit. He can crack any code and nothing is too technological for him. The gadgets he uses are very advanced and like nothing you've seen before.

DESIGN CONCEPT

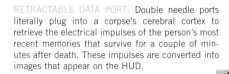

★

RETRACTABLE DATA PORT: Double needle ports literally plug into a corpse's cerebral cortex to retrieve the electrical impulses of the person's most recent memories that survive for a couple of minutes after death. These impulses are converted into images that appear on the HUD.

Brawler

Model: Attack vehicle
Code Name: Brawler
Engine: Turbodiesel

★ Equipped with a state of the art communications/computer terminal, the Brawler armored van is equal parts attack vehicle and mobile command center. The heightened roof allows for ease of movement in the rear compartment. Computer terminals link up with G.I. JOE tracker beacons to locate operatives anywhere in the world. The utility vehicle is designed for off-road and city driving.

★ CANNONS: Roof mounted cannons are collapsible for low profile missions.

★ DASHBOARD: Personal touches on the dashboard create cover for the Brawler as a recreational vehicle

SEATING: Folding bench seats provide versatility in troop or materials transport.

DESIGN CONCEPT

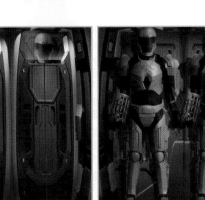

★ INTERIOR STORAGE: Hooks on the rear panel are specifically designed to transport accelerator suits.

DEFEND PARIS

Objective: ★ Engage enemy operatives and minimize damage to the city and its inhabitants
Location: ★ Paris, France
Team Assigned: ★ G.I. JOE Team Alpha
Hostile: ★ Forces under the command of James McCullen
Status: ★ Concluded

G.I. JOE Team Alpha was ordered to Paris after the female operative in the Kyrgyzstan engagement was determined to be Baroness Anastasia DeCobray, wife of Baron Daniel DeCobray. The Baron is a noted French scientist working on the particle accelerator project, an integral component in weaponizing the nanotech warheads. The initial plan to enter the DeCobray facility and capture the enemy was aborted when MARS operatives exited the building and came face to face with Team Alpha. The enemy's unlikely escape path through the city indicated that it was heading toward a destination, rather than simply fleeing the G.I. JOE unit. A quick calculation of the vehicle's path suggested a potential target. A decision in the field was made to change the mission objective to prevent enemy agents from deploying their weapon. The city incurred considerable damage during the engagement as combatants battled through numerous locations across town.

JoAnn Perritano (co-producer/unit production manager): I've shot in Paris before and it's a wonderful city, but there's lots of red tape. It's very difficult. There's a lot of traffic. We just couldn't do the kinds of things in Paris that the script called for: flipping cars up in the air and blowing things up, shutting down the streets and re-routing traffic. It just wasn't the city for that. So the next best thing was, "What has a Paris feel? What can we make look like Paris but still get all of the permissions and be able to do the kinds of things that we needed to do on this movie?" And Prague came to mind. It's similar. You've got the cobblestone streets and then in comes the art department with some signage and street signs and all that. And, hopefully, when you're actually watching the car explode, you're not going to realize that you're not in Paris, if we did our job right.

David Womark (executive producer): One of the streets we shot at is essentially like Rodeo Drive in Beverly Hills. They let us lock it down, put our cars in there, and shoot cars. You'd show up on the set and sometimes the second unit is outside people's apartments—there's the set! A Hummer flying seventy-five feet in the air, landing inches from its target. Sometimes it felt to us like a back lot, but part of the challenge for our special effects supervisor, Dan Sudick—who's done a lot of Mr. Spielberg's movies, *Indiana Jones*, *War of the Worlds*, and is used to doing a lot of these effects either in a back lot or on a sound stage—is that all of a sudden he finds himself throwing cars in front of people's houses. You want to make sure that the car doesn't land in somebody's living room....

Greg Michael (second unit director): The Hummer is equipped with, basically, a cowcatcher; something that you would find on the front of a locomotive. At high speeds, this cowcatcher can get under the back of a car, or the front of a car, and send that car flying into the sky. For the last week and a half, we have been flipping, flying, floating, and crashing as many cars as we can. I think we have eighty-six cars on this movie. In one day we destroyed seventeen. So that was a pretty good number. There was one shot in particular, which hopefully we have footage of. We have what we call the "aircraft carrier," which is basically an eighteen-wheel flatbed truck. We had three cars on flippers, and those cars were flipped forty feet in the air. The idea is that we're tracking behind our black Hummer, and from the back of the Hummer, all you see is just these cars flipping as if they've been hit by this cowcatcher. But when it's all cut together, it's going to look like that Hummer actually is plowing through traffic and just knocking these cars flying through the air, left and right. It should be quite spectacular.

Stephen Sommers (director): Every movie I make there's usually one really big chase sequence. There's a lot of great action sequences, but *this* is a big chase sequence. Our villains have a state of the art vehicle and they have something that our heroes want. Basically we race through and rip up Paris. It was really fun. Obviously, our heroes have to be aware there can be no civilian casualties. They are very careful about that.

We've done New York to death. Everybody's always blowing up poor old New York. This takes place all over the world and there's a reason that we end up in Paris. But it was very complicated. It took thousands of hours and storyboarding and pre-vizing and trying to figure it all out. The whole team has to get together to discuss every single cut, every single shot, because it involves mechanical effects and visual effects and stunt people and the entire motor pool.

Bob Ducsay (producer): Dan Sudick is the physical effects guy. He had the opportunity of launching a lot of cars into the air and a lot of big explosions and things like that that we did practically. For all the massive visual effects that are in the movie, we also actually got to do a lot of things on location. And that's also really fun. It's exciting to actually see these things happen and to get them on film without having to go and spend a bunch of money on visual effects.

Ed Verreaux (production designer): We'll be using a tremendous amount of visual effects in this movie to extend sets, to make sets look bigger, to make stuff that maybe doesn't quite look right—you know, look like we're in Paris. Even though Prague is a beautiful European city, it's very gothic, very old-world. It really doesn't look exactly like Paris. And so there probably will be a couple of places where we're going to have to add a little bit of Paris. Certainly, we have a whole sequence of shots where we're seeing the Eiffel Tower in the distance, and that doesn't exist here. So we'll be adding that, if nothing else.

Delta-6 Accelerator Suit

⭐ The Delta-6 accelerator suit is a mechanical exoskeleton with head to toe turbo-hydraulics and highly pressurized pneumatics to enhance the wearer's ability to run faster, jump higher, and hit harder than humanly possible. The flexible poly-alloy suit provides lightweight, bulletproof battle armor that allows the wearer to punch through solid obstacles as dense as a brick wall. The suit also boasts an impressive weapons system of fully self-contained firepower.

Each suit costs millions of dollars to construct, so special care should be taken when wearing.

DESIGN CONCEPT

⭐ The right arm boasts a 10mm caseless Gatling submachine gun, a six-barreled automatic weapon capable of firing fifty rounds per second. Targeting is achieved with the wrist-top laser sight.

▶ **DESIGN ANALYSIS**

Ellen Mirojnick (costume designer): The accelerator suit was one of the first concept suits that were drawn, by a terrific concept artist by the name of Matt Codd. What happens when you do concept art to when you actually have to make the costume or make the garment, it's a million miles away.

We commissioned the suit to Shane Mahan at Stan Winston Studios to actualize and we contributed to helping him turn this two-dimensional image into a three-dimensional suit. You think about somebody wearing a Ferrari or the fastest machine known to mankind, and that's what the accelerator suit will be.

⭐ Hydraulically enhanced titanium boots fit over the shoes to increase running speed to approximately sixty miles per hour. While cobalt machine parts snap into place over the arms and legs, allowing for extra power.

▶ DESIGN ANALYSIS

Stephen Sommers (director): I actually wrote a script about ten or twelve years ago called 'Accelerator.' The whole script was based on this piece of gear. It was really cool, but I didn't sell the script. When this came up I said, "I know where this goes."

We don't like losing our guys. We respect our men and women in uniform and we hate when we lose them. The idea of the future is that you can see how weaponry and the military are going. They're trying to make it as casualty free as possible. They're going to have a version of the accelerator suit where our guys are as hard to kill as possible. The accelerator suits are basically the armor of the future.

HELMET

The ultra-lightweight accelerator helmet has a visor with an advanced cybernetics heads-up display (HUD). The transparent display relays laser enhanced LED readouts for scanning and communications information.

★ Vents with intake and exhaust fans circulate air to maintain temperature and oxygen flow.

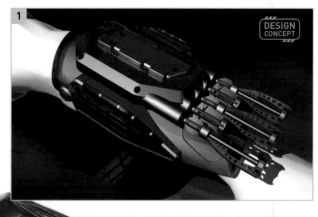

★

LEFT ARM CARTRIDGES:

1. Three gas-propelled grappling spears with spring loaded, titanium-tipped barbs.

2. Five 25mm high-explosive, heat-seeking "fire-and-forget" wrist rockets.

Shane Mahan (accelerator suit SFX designer): If you actually were to make it as heavy as it really appears, it would be about 200 or 300 pounds, which would be the non-accelerator suit! It would be the suit that doesn't allow the actors to perform properly, because these suits were actually meant to be used for running shots and other actions.

Marlon Wayans (Ripcord): If hell was a costume, it'd be the accelerator suit. The devil probably has an accelerator suit or two in his closet. He has a black one and a green one. I don't like it, but I'm an actor and it's what I do. The audience will never know that I hate that suit.

Nano-Mites

★ Nano-mites are microscopic robots that work together to perform tasks on a molecular level. They were originally created with the beneficial applications of isolating and destroying cancer cells in mind. However, MARS Industries—under funding from NATO—discovered ways to program nano-mites for a variety of less altruistic tasks, such as destroying metal compounds. It is believed that MARS Industries has been working for a decade on this technology at a cost of approximately €13 billion. However, their greatest advancement in the development of this technology has occurred in the past four years.

Tests conducted on the body of an enemy agent that attacked G.I. JOE headquarters revealed that nano-mite technology has been used on human test subjects to increase speed, agility, and resilience. It has also been adapted into a form of mind control.

Theoretically, nano-mites injected into the human body could even be programmed to reshape a person's appearance, reforming facial bones, changing the texture and elasticity of skin, and even changing eye color.

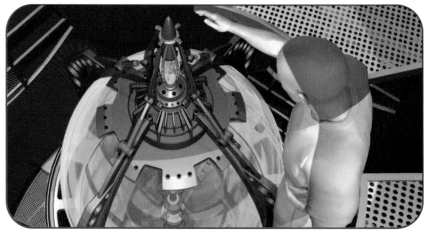

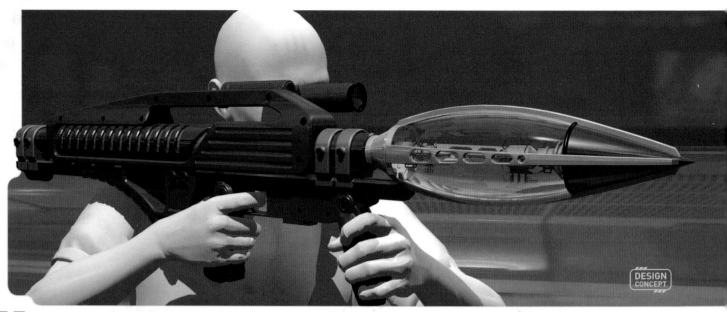

DESIGN CONCEPT

DESIGN CONCEPT

22.66

29.33

The warheads are stored in a secured MARS weapon case that opens with the code 529440. The code also activates a secondary tracking device.

42.96

20.17

M.A.R.S.

DESIGN CONCEPT

NANOTECH WARHEADS

Nanotech warheads were the first practical application of the new nano-mite technology. MARS Industries created an initial shipment of four weapons to be delivered to NATO forces. Each nanotech warhead contains seven million nano-mites with the ability to eat any metal, from a single tank to an entire city, with no direct human casualties. They can be either fired from a shoulder-mounted missile or carried on a rocket for delivery to distant targets. A particle accelerator is required to activate the nanotech warheads with electrically charged atoms.

A kill switch, unique to each warhead, deactivates the nano-mites, short-circuiting them to prevent any unwanted destruction. Each kill switch is a short-range device, required to be in relatively close proximity to the nano-mites to deactivate them.

PARTICLE ACCELERATOR: Uses electric fields to propel electrically-charged particles to high speeds and to contain them. The device is usually used in particle physics.

DESIGN CONCEPT

Parti
Dark

Stuart Beattie (screenplay writer): We wanted to find a story that could only exist in the world of G.I. JOE, and not in any other. Couldn't exist in James Bond or *Mission: Impossible*, or any of those other films. It had to be a G.I. JOE story. So we found out about these little microscopic robots that destroy anything you want them to and hit upon that as a very G.I. JOE thing. Once we came up with that, then you've got the small portable suitcase, the McGuffin that everyone's after. Then it's just a matter of that changing hands until it gets to the end and they get used. I was very determined to keep the plot simple. I'm not a big fan of these complex plots where you don't know who's doing what, or who's on who's side. I'm very much a fan of simple stories with complex characters.

Joseph Gordon-Levitt (the Doctor): I've actually been learning a bit about what nanotechnology really is. G.I. JOE presents a fantastic, larger than life, picture of nanotechnology, but it's based on something that's actually really happening. They are building machines that are so microscopic that they can engineer things on a molecular level. At this point, they can't do it fast enough to make anything out of it, but they can go in and take an atom off of a molecule and put it on a different molecule. It's just a matter of time before they can make machines that can do that fast enough where soon they'll be able to have these little nano-mites that can build anything—that can turn garbage into strawberries, or can clean our air or cure diseases or all these really great things. And, as is presented in G.I. JOE, maybe they could also make some dangerous weapons. That's up to us in the future to see to it that this super powerful technology gets put to good use instead of put to evil use.

MARS
Scarab

Model: Attack truck
Code Name: Scarab

★ The Scarab bulletproof attack truck comes equipped with an interior computer console, fully-concealed weapons system, and optional roof rack. In camouflage mode, the Scarab looks like a high-end sport utility vehicle, but this vehicle is loaded down with a battle-ready heavy weapons system.

TIRES: Puncture-resistant tires are able to withstand multiple bullet strikes. They refill and reseal immediately following any inflicted damage.

CANON: Pulse canon emerges from rooftop panel with a horizontal rotation of 360 degrees.

COWCATCHER: Retractable steel "shovel" emerges from the grill to clear debris from the vehicle's path.

PANELS: Side panels contain retractable missile racks controlled from the onboard computer console. Targeting scanner can lock onto objects either ahead of or behind the vehicle.

SCARLETT

Name: ★ Shana O'Hara
Call Sign: ★ Scarlett
Rank: ★ Sergeant
Nationality: ★ American
Specialization: ★ Counterintelligence. Linguistics
Current Assignment: ★ G.I. JOE Team Alpha
Previous Assignment: ★ U.S. Military Intelligence
Observations of Note: ★ "Attraction is an emotion. Emotions are not based in science. And if you can't quantify or prove that something exists, well, in my mind... it doesn't."

Shana 'Scarlett' O'Hara possesses a genius level I.Q. that, combined with a dedication to learning, allowed her to graduate college at a young age. Besides her specialization in counterintelligence, Scarlett possesses a secondary skill set in the ninja arts as a result of her training with Snake-Eyes. She is the current record holder for the terrorist obstacle course in the Urban Combat Level.

Scarlett keeps up to date on all scientific and militaristic research and development.

▶ PSYCHOLOGICAL PROFILE

Rachel Nichols (Scarlett): I have to say, Scarlett was even cooler than I had imagined. I mean she's the girl in a sea of JOEs that are men.... She's always been a girl that can keep up with the boys. She can play with the boys. She can hang with the boys. And they all have to listen to her, because she's the only girl. Which is great on set, because all the boys have to listen to Rachel, because she's the only girl!

Crossbow Pistol

★ The gas propulsion crossbow pistol fires long-range laser arrow bolts that can electrocute a human target.

▶ **WEAPON ANALYSIS**

Brad Einhorn (property master): It scares you when it opens, because you're not expecting it to open. It looks almost like a magic trick. I think when you see the movie, you could almost think it's a CG effect, but it isn't. It's really a practical crossbow that opens.

Pistol closed

Pistol holstered

DESIGN CONCEPT

Rachel Nichols: The crossbow comes up, and those two lasers come out on the side. It doesn't actually fire. They had to make the weapon entirely, and they couldn't safely make it where the lasers would come out of the side, and then they could actually fire blanks. They were worried that it would get stuck and jammed. We're going to pretend it fires, and it's going to look like it fires in the movie, but it doesn't fire really. Which makes it easy for me actually, because then I can never miss a target. Scarlett hits every target the first time, because we add the gunfire after the movie's over.

★ A built-in camera in the viewfinder is able to record a photograph of a target. The LED screen can be programmed to fire a Smart-Arrow that hones in on the actual target of that image even when the crossbow is aimed in a different direction.

★ Laser arrow bolts cannot pierce all forms of body armor, but they are effective at cutting through lightweight metal.

Arrow bolt's wing mechanism

MISSION 1.4:

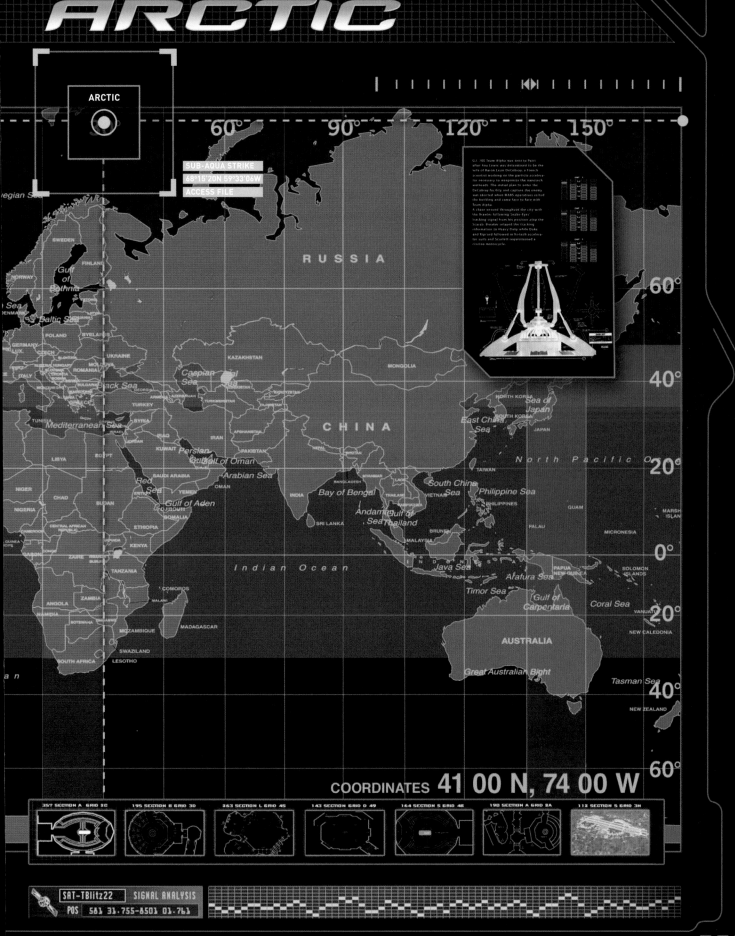

ARCTIC

SUB-AQUA STRIKE
68°15'20N 59°33'06W
ACCESS FILE

G.I. JOE Team Alpha was sent to Paris after Ana Lewis was determined to be the wife of Baron Leon DeCobray, a French scientist working on the particle accelerator necessary to reweapon the nanotech warheads. The initial plan to enter the DeCobray facility and capture the enemy was aborted when MARS operatives raided the building and came face to face with Team Alpha.

A chase ensued throughout the city with the Brawler following Snake-Eyes' tracking signal from his position atop the Scarab. Breaker relayed the tracking information to Heavy Duty while Duke and Ripcord followed in hi-tech accelerator suits and Scarlett requisitioned a civilian motorcycle.

60° | 90° | 120° | 150°

NORWEGIAN Sea

SWEDEN
FINLAND
NORWAY
Gulf of Bothnia

RUSSIA

DENMARK
Baltic Sea
GERMANY
LUX.
POLAND
BYELARUS
CZECH
ITALY
MOLDOVA
ROMANIA
UKRAINE
KAZAKHSTAN
MONGOLIA
Black Sea
GEORGIA
TURKEY
ARMENIA AZERBAIJAN
TURKMENISTAN
UZBEKISTAN
KYRGYZSTAN
TAJIKISTAN
Mediterranean Sea
SYRIA
ISRAEL
IRAQ
IRAN
AFGHANISTAN

CHINA

60°
40°
NORTH KOREA
SOUTH KOREA
Sea of Japan
East China Sea
JAPAN

TUNISIA
LIBYA
EGYPT
JORDAN
KUWAIT
Persian Gulf of Oman
SAUDI ARABIA
PAKISTAN
BHUTAN

Red Sea
YEMEN
OMAN
Arabian Sea
INDIA
MYANMAR
LAOS
Bay of Bengal
THAILAND
CAMBODIA
VIETNAM
South China Sea
Philippine Sea
TAIWAN

20°

NIGER
CHAD
SUDAN
NIGERIA
ETHIOPIA
SRI LANKA
Andaman Gulf of Sea Thailand
MALAYSIA
BRUNEI
PHILIPPINES
GUAM
PALAU
MARSHALL ISLANDS

North Pacific Ocean

CENTRAL AFRICAN REPUBLIC
GUINEA
GABON
ZAIRE
KENYA
BURUNDI
TANZANIA

Java Sea
PAPUA NEW GUINEA
MICRONESIA

0°

ANGOLA
ZAMBIA
MALAWI
COMOROS
Indian Ocean
Arafura Sea
Timor Sea
SOLOMON ISLANDS

20°

NAMIBIA
BOTSWANA
MOZAMBIQUE
MADAGASCAR
Gulf of Carpentaria
Coral Sea
VANUATU
NEW CALEDONIA

SWAZILAND
SOUTH AFRICA
LESOTHO

AUSTRALIA

Great Australian Bight

40°

Tasman Sea
NEW ZEALAND

60°

COORDINATES 41 00 N, 74 00 W

357 SECTION A GRID 2C | 195 SECTION B GRID 3D | 263 SECTION L GRID 4S | 143 SECTION G GRID D 49 | 164 SECTION S GRID 4B | 190 SECTION A GRID 3A | 112 SECTION S GRID 3N

MARS

Designation: Military Armaments
Research Syndicate
Alternate Designation: MARS
Industries
Head of Organization: James
McCullen (Founder/CEO)
Industry: Armament Solutions

 The Military Armaments Research
Syndicate, under the leadership
of CEO James 'Destro' McCullen, is a
global leader in technological research
and development. MARS Industries
specializes in weapons development
ranging from personal firearms to
assault vehicles favored by NATO. Their
scientists are continually developing
cutting-edge technology, including the
recent groundbreaking work with nano-
mites which are sure to have far reach-
ing implications beyond military use.

The MARS brand logo can be found
on bunkers and buildings as well as
personal technology used in everyday life. This multinational company
employs thousands of workers across
the world in major metropolises and
burgeoning Third World countries.
The work being done by MARS
Industries contributes to the global
economy in ways that cannot be fully
quantified, but they are clearly an
emerging leader in the balance of
power between nations.

MARS WEAPONS FACTORY

One of the many MARS Industries holdings is the Central Asia factory in Kyrgyzstan. The factory is an ultra-secure location where much of MARS' most secret designs are produced. The factory is protected by an advanced alarm system, and security guards throughout the complex are armed with the latest in MARS weaponry, making it a near-impenetrable fortress. No technology or research has ever been stolen from the facility.

ARCTIC BASE

Objective: ★ Unknown
Location: ★ Beneath the Polar Ice Cap
Levels: ★ Unknown
Status: ★ Destroyed at conclusion
of MISSION 1.4: ARCTIC

DESIGN CONCEPT

McCullen's secret headquarters, built into the seabed under the Polar Ice Cap, is an advanced stronghold befitting the top weapons designer in the world. Nearly undetectable and highly defensible, the base is heavily armed with cutting-edge MARS weaponry, including harpoon guns and a turbo-pulse cannon.

A landing strip on the ice above leads into a cave where MARS vehicles can be stored to avoid aerial reconnaissance. Hidden behind an ice wall façade is a hi-tech diving bell that takes passengers from the surface down to

the underwater facility on a deep sea elevator cable system. The diving bell entry port is under constant guard by a pair of Neo-Vipers. A secondary entrance is located in the base itself where watertight doors open into an enormous docking bay capable of holding several vessels, including a submarine.

The ultra-modern facility has the technological capabilities necessary for McCullen to command his small army, complete with a self-destruct protocol that will bring down the ice pack above it to destroy all evidence of his plans.

▶ **DESIGN ANALYSIS**

Ed Verreaux (production designer): In the first big meeting we had with Hasbro, when they were introducing us to the brand, they said that the bad guys have the really cool designs. They have the real slick design stuff. And the JOEs' stuff is a little bit more utilitarian, a little bit more everyday military. So we've kept that. You'll see the MARS gun ship, the Night Raven, and it's pretty slick and kind of sexy. You'll see the way the Baroness dresses. That's not to say that Scarlett doesn't look great in her liquid armor, because she does, but the JOE stuff's a little bit more utilitarian, not quite so over-designed, or designed in a slick way. The villains' stuff is a little bit fancier.

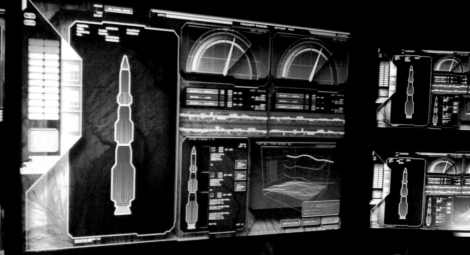

FLIGHT CONTROL ROOM

The flight control room serves as the command hub for the MARS underwater base. Looking out over the docking bay entrance through the Perspex windows, security can visually track entry to and departure from the facility through the watertight doors. Security protocols are routed through the control room, allowing access to the base's impressive defensive and early warning system. From here, pilots can control aerial attack drones carrying dangerous cargo.

Kate Sullivan (set decorator): The MARS base is under the Polar Ice Cap and the G.I. JOE base is underground somewhere out in the desert. In the MARS base there were more environmental monitoring devices to measure air quality, environmental systems and whether there was a leak in the roof, like on a submarine. Everything in MARS was cool grey and blues with minimal accents of other colors. The Pit was more traditional military with military colors and military dressing. MARS was more a warren of tunnels and intersecting rooms, while The Pit was a series of tunnels that connected to gigantic underground spaces. We had to fill those spaces, which was much more challenging because there was a lot more to fill.

VERTICAL LAUNCH BAYS

Smart Drones launched from these vertical bays can reach target points thousands of miles away. Heat from the launch melts the ice at the top of each bay, providing a clear path for the drones to exit. The ice reforms within minutes of the launch to minimize access to the underground facility.

Access corridors leading to the bays allow workers to prepare the drones for launch. Once the launch sequence commences, the entry hatches seal shut to keep rocket fire from entering the facility. When not in use, security protocols on the access corridors activate the laser protection and pressure plating in the floor. If anything larger than a quarter touches the floor it will be electrocuted.

Turbo-Pulse Cannon

★ The automated phased array turbo-pulse battery is the main gun defending the underwater base. Laser conduits converge on the cannon control room where a pair of technicians operate the gun. The cannon pivots a full 180 degrees to lock onto a target.

The laser control core is an energy shaft beneath the laser control room. It serves as the main conduit for the ten energy lasers that feed into the gun. The shaft bottoms out in the arctic water to keep the machinery super-cooled.

▶ DESIGN ANALYSIS

Ed Verreaux: One of the [sets] that was the most fun was the laser control room and laser control core.... There's this big shaft with this big laser that fires a laser cannon that, in the third act, is an important part of the story. Snake-Eyes and Storm Shadow also have their final duel in this space. It was really a fun set because it was about five stories high and fairly large and there was a huge action sequence that takes place in it.

What happened for me with a lot of these was we had to do them so quickly that we really didn't have much time to really think about it. We had to go ahead as fast as we could. Sometimes, as the sets would come to fruition, I would be watching them very carefully, hoping that this is going to work out. Then the company would get there and the lighting would be done, and they'd photograph it, and they'd say, "You know, this looks really good." It's been a whole series of good events like that.

DESIGN CONCEPT

Operating Chamber

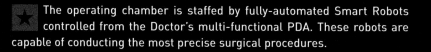

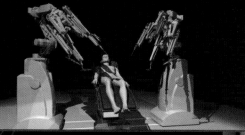

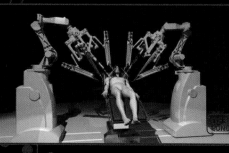

⭐ The operating chamber is staffed by fully-automated Smart Robots controlled from the Doctor's multi-functional PDA. These robots are capable of conducting the most precise surgical procedures.

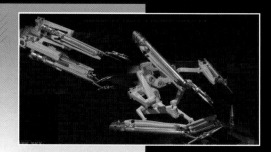

DESIGN CONCEPT ///

DESIGN CONCEPT ///

MARS Submarine

Model: Submarine
Powered By: Nuclear reactor
Speed: Surface: 12 Knots; Submerged: 25+ Knots
Operating Depth: Greater than 1,000 feet

★ The MARS Industries nuclear powered stealth submarine is capable of traversing arctic waters. The submarine's interior is designed for comfort as much as practicality; looking more like a private office than part of an underwater vessel.

DESIGN CONCEPT

DESIGN CONCEPT

MARS spear guns

STORM SHADOW

Name: ★ Thomas S. Arashikage
Alias: ★ Storm Shadow
Profession: ★ Ninja assassin

Young Thomas S. Arashikage was a standout student in the ninja arts at the temple of his father, Hard Master, until the day a young Snake-Eyes arrived. The two boys formed an uneasy partnership, training together, with Storm Shadow usually managing to gain the upper hand. As their training progressed, Snake-Eyes' skills began to match those of his contemporary, until one day Storm Shadow met defeat at the hands of his sparring partner.

Storm Shadow now works as a freelance ninja assassin, following a strict honor code that—among other things—forbids him from killing women. Nevertheless, he is a skilled killer, with moves so quick that, at times, he can seem to disappear. Storm Shadow nurses his rivalry with Snake-Eyes to this day. Recent events have seen these "brothers" facing each other again in battle.

▶ **PSYCHOLOGICAL PROFILE**
Lorenzo di Bonaventura (producer): Storm Shadow and Snake-Eyes are really the stuff of legends. From the first time they meet at ten years old, to the time in this movie, they have been pitted against one another. They have lived under the same roof, and they have a blood vendetta that is based on a deeply-felt wrong.

SHURIKEN: Japanese throwing stars are multi-pointed, concealed weapons. The name literally translates to 'sword hidden in the hand.'

KATANA

Curved, single-edge Japanese sword. Storm Shadow has a specially-forged pair of blades that can be linked together to form an extended sword.

DESIGN CONCEPT

★ HOLSTER: Storm Shadow carries his swords in a custom-made double-katana holster.

PULSE PISTOL

Like the Baroness, Storm Shadow carries a customised pulse pistol, though he favors unarmed combat and his traditional ninja weapons.

Name: ★ Unknown
Call Sign: ★ Snake-Eyes
Rank: ★ Master Sergeant
Nationality: ★ American
Specialization: ★ Covert operations
Current Assignment: ★ G.I. JOE Team Alpha
Previous Assignment: ★ Classified

Snake-Eyes has been training in the ways of the ninja for most of his life. He is skilled with a variety of traditional weapons for hand-to-hand combat as well as modern firearms. With his specialized expertise in martial arts and espionage, he is the ultimate one-man strike team.

Living on the streets of Tokyo at age ten, Snake-Eyes was taken in by Hard Master of the Arashikage Temple. He trained with Hard Master's son, Tommy Arashikage (alias: Storm Shadow), until the day that young Snake-Eyes was skilled enough to win in a fight against the boy.

DESIGN
CONCEPT

COMMUNICATOR
As Snake-Eyes does not
speak, this device is used
for long-range communica-
tion with the other members
of Team Alpha.

UTILITY KNIFE
This custom-made knife consists of two interlocking blades, each with a stabbing point and razor sharp cutting edge.

★

CYBER TONFAS: Traditionally used in pairs, this impact weapon runs the length of the forearm. A pair of contained blades eject from the end of this model.

▶**PSYCHOLOGICAL PROFILE**

Ray Park (Snake-Eyes): I knew all about Snake-Eyes growing up. I knew all about Storm Shadow. I really wanted to do the movie because of the fans and because of my younger brother and me playing with that big twelve-inch doll as boys.... Snake-Eyes doesn't speak. That interests me, as an actor, because I really like to use my body in a physical way. The less speaking, the better.

★

WEAPONS BELT: Contains a variety of weapons and equipment traditional to the ninja.

KATANA

Curved, single-edge Japanese sword, often associated with a samurai.

★

CAMOUFLAGE VISOR: Changes color to match traditional black uniform or white survival suit.

★

BRAND: Red markings on his sword and right triceps signify that Snake-Eyes is a member of the Arashikage Ninja Clan.

★

GLOCK PISTOL: "Safe action" sidearm that can fire a wide range of ammunition and is popular with military and law enforcement agencies.

Arashikage Ninja Clan

★ Snake-Eyes was taken in by the secretive Arashikage Clan when he was ten years old. He received his early training from Hard Master, who quickly recognized and nurtured the boy's talent. Hard Master is also rumoured to have given his young pupil, who's origins and real name remain unknown, his clan name, Snake-Eyes.

▶ **HISTORICAL ANALYSIS**

R.A. Rondell (stunt coordinator): We found these two kids that were really, really talented. We brought them in and it was a pleasure to work with them, because they were so professional and so talented. We started working out little fights with them and we actually had to bring in two additional doubles for each one of the children because we could only work them five hours at a time. So we actually had six kids all together.

Fight coordinator Marcus Young trained all six of them to do a fight in the kitchen, and each one of the kids could do any of the fights any of the time. We'd line them all up, and bring in the first set of kids—the doubles—and they would do the lineups for camera while the actor kids would wait and then they would come in and they would shoot. Then we'd pull them out and we'd bring the other set of kids that would do more of

the insert work, so we could rotate them and keep them on their five hour school schedules.

Each one of the kids was completely trained, knew the fights inside and out, and was very supportive of the other pair that were fighting at the same time. There were no jealousies or animosities. They sat back as a little group. It was a complete team of nine-year-old kids.

Stephen Sommers (director): Snake-Eyes is everybody's favorite character and he doesn't talk. That makes it really, really hard [to film], but I didn't want to let the audience down. For me it wasn't just about coming up with the greatest ninja fight ever. He's one of many characters and we're not going to spend three months just doing a ninja fight. That's not what the movie's about. But we have to make sure that everybody who loves Snake-Eyes is getting everything they want out of him for one movie. That's when we came up with the idea that it's an origin story.

We thought, "Let's start showing where Snake-Eyes came from; that he was an orphan and taken in. How he learned his martial arts and how his enmity with Storm Shadow began." We wanted to create him from the beginning. I think it makes the movie much more fun.

G.I. JOE Submarine

Model: G.I. JOE submarine
Powered By: Nuclear reactor
Speed: Surface: 12 Knots; Submerged: 25+ Knots
Operating Depth: Greater than 1,000 feet

★ The G.I. JOE submarine is capable of navigating in arctic waters at extreme depths. The submarine carries a large crew compliment and a variety of underwater and surface attack vehicles. The reinforced outer hull is strong enough to break through an icepack with little to no damage to the sub.

★ CONN: The conn (control room) command center is the hub for communications, surveillance, and submarine defenses. Computers are equipped with 3D mapping technology and link to a mini robotic underwater spy system.

LAUNCH PORTS
Two-person submersible SHARC units attach to launch ports on the exterior of the submarine.

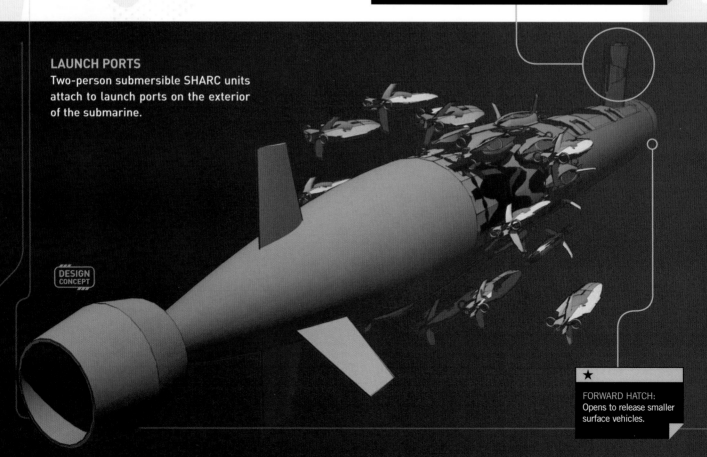

DESIGN CONCEPT

★ FORWARD HATCH: Opens to release smaller surface vehicles.

Sharc

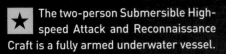

Model: Submersible attack vehicle
Code Name: SHARC

★ The two-person Submersible High-speed Attack and Reconnaissance Craft is a fully armed underwater vessel.

DESIGN CONCEPT

★

COCKPIT: Separate sections house a pilot and a gunner for independent navigation and defense.

MINI ROBOTIC UNDERWATER SPY SYSTEM
Designed as the perfect undersea camouflage, the mini robotic underwater spy system mimics the appearance and movement of a fish while feeding video and scanning information back to computers onboard the submarine.

ARCTIC ATTACK

Objective: ★ Infiltrate enemy base.
Location: ★ Beneath the Polar Ice Cap
Team Assigned: ★ Multiple rogue G.I. JOE strike teams
Hostile: ★ Forces under the command of James McCullen
Status: ★ Concluded

As a result of cutting-edge technological interrogation techniques on an enemy agent, G.I. JOE operatives were able to determine the general location of the secret MARS base at the Polar Ice Cap. Additional assistance provided by a JOE operative at the base allowed the incoming team to pinpoint the exact coordinates and mount their attack on the facility. Heavy Duty led the battlefront from the SHARC underwater attack vehicles,

while the rest of G.I. JOE Team Alpha infiltrated the base on a rescue and recovery mission. Prior to entering the facility mission parameters changed, necessitating an altering of the plan as the infiltration team split up to cover multiple prongs of the operation. Once inside the base, G.I. JOE operatives engaged enemy agents in one-on-one engagements while an underwater battle raged outside the facility.

Survival Suit

Model: Survival suit
Function: Insulation, protection
and camouflage

★ G.I. JOE survival suits are designed to blend into a snowy environment while keeping operatives protected and preventing hypothermia in extreme cold temperatures. Neoprene underarmor combined with an arctic-rated parka and insulated snowpants allow for comfort and flexibility of movement.

Rock Slide

Model: Polar assault vehicle
Code Name: Rock Slide
Powered By: Four Stroke engine

★ Fully armed, high performance snow-mobile built for evasive maneuvering and ease of travel through virgin terrain.

★ WEAPONRY: Armed with heat-seeking rockets and dual machine guns

★ WINDSHIELD: Bulletproof windshield with aerodynamic design protects the driver from attack and the elements while lessening drag caused by wind resistance.

★ TRACK: Kevlar track propels the vehicle at high speeds over ice and snow.

▶ MISSION ANALYSIS

Ray Park (Snake-Eyes): With this movie I'm working with a team of guys—R.A. Rondell is the stunt coordinator, Marcus Young is the fight coordinator. Marcus has his own team, and those guys are so good. They're from different styles of martial arts. My style is very different from theirs. Not to say that it's better or worse. [My style,] Wushu, is more of a flamboyant style and they understand that. We combine what I can do with what they wanted me to show and bring it together and just sort of dance with it and play with it. We worked together on it but I'm not the one who's choreographing fights. That's a big responsibility. It has been really good to have the A-team there to work out the beats and say, "Hey, Ray, this is what we've got planned for here." I would step in and go, "This doesn't feel quite right, can I do this? Can I do that?" We'd get together and tie it in to make it look as good as we can for ourselves. The training I've had to do for this has been unbelievable.

R.A. Rondell (stunt coordinator): Ray Park comes from a huge martial arts background. That was one of the strong points for him. He's got this Wushu style that's really amazing. The head postures and the hand postures and the poses are what the audience wants to see, because that's Snake-Eyes. This is the first time I had met Byung-hun Lee [Storm Shadow]. He's a huge star in Korea. A martial artist. He brings his own quality to it as well. He's a little bit more methodical and stylish in his way. But when you put them both together, it's quite a battle. They both really excel at their martial arts. I think their styles really compliment each other.

MARS *TRANSPORT*

Night Raven

Model: Attack jet
Code Name: Night Raven

⭐ The Night Raven jet flies at supersonic speeds and is capable of high altitude flight. It can be maneuvered with precision even while flying in the upper atmosphere.

The plane's flight controls include a voice-activated weapons system linked to the pilot's flight helmet. Commands must be relayed in the Celtic language.

//Fire command: *Teine*
//Eject command: *Cur magh*

DESIGN CONCEPT

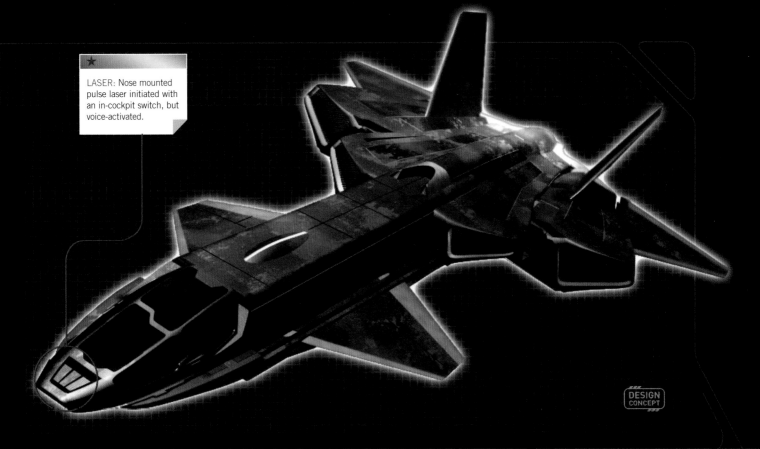

LASER: Nose mounted pulse laser initiated with an in-cockpit switch, but voice-activated.

DESIGN CONCEPT

HEADS-UP DISPLAY

Cockpit flight control instrument panel automatically activates when the pilot takes up position and flight goggles with integrated control interface automatically position over the pilot's face.

DESIGN CONCEPT

EJECTION HELMET: A helmet with integrated oxygen mask automatically drops over the pilot's head when the ejection sequence is activated.

DESIGN CONCEPT

Mantis

Model: Mini-submarine
Code Name: Mantis

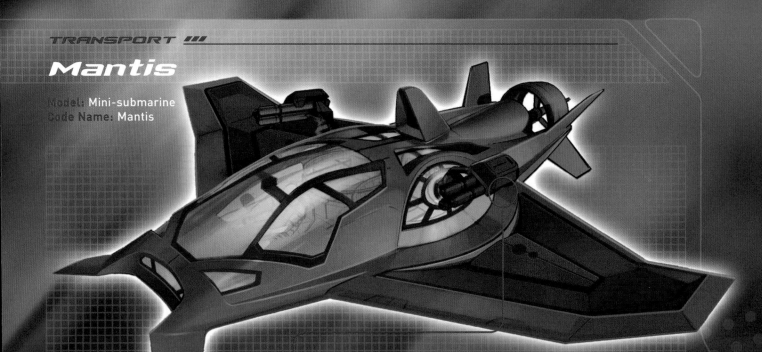

DESIGN CONCEPT ///

★ CANNON: Multiple harpoon cannons fire harpoon torpedoes.

★ The two-person Mantis underwater attack craft is a sleek, high performance submarine that seats a pilot and gunner for independent navigation and firing controls.

THE DOCTOR

Name: ★ Unknown
Alias: ★ The Doctor
Nationality: ★ American
Profession: ★ Research scientist
Specialization: ★ Nano-mite technology

Little is known about the twisted genius behind MARS research and development who goes by the moniker "The Doctor." He is credited with creating the nano-mite technology used in MARS Industries' most advanced weapons development. It is believed that he based his experiments on the research of others, taking the technology into previously unimaginable, and horrifying, directions. Scarred beyond recognition from a previous accident, the Doctor relies on a portable life-support system to keep himself alive.

▶ PSYCHOLOGICAL PROFILE

Joseph Gordon-Levitt (the Doctor): The Doctor started out as a good guy. Really smart guy. Gifted, incredible scientific mind. And things kind of go awry.... His good intentions turn into a bit of megalomania. And like all good villains he thinks the world would be a better place if he were in charge.

The bad guy's always the most fun to play. Chan[ning Tatum] is mad jealous of what I get to do. Whenever I talk to Chan, he's like, "Man, you get to do all the fun stuff." I was like, "You're right. That's no coincidence chump, I took the job for a reason!"

NANO-MITE INJECTORS
The Doctor carries portable versions of the nano-mite injectors with him at all times.

DESIGN CONCEPT

LIFE SUPPORT MASK:
The Doctor's mask
continually pumps air
into his lungs in place
of a failing respiratory
system.

MECHANICAL LARYNX:
assists with speech,
compensating for
missing vocal cords.